IMPLEMENTOR

EVERY LEADER NEEDS TO KNOW HOW TO DO AN EXTRAORDINARY TRANSFORMATION OF PEOPLE BY BRIDGING DIFFERENCES FOR BETTER MENTORING AND CREATING VALUE IN OTHER PEOPLE'S LIVES.

DR. AMIT DAS

To

All my bosses who made a difference in my professional career.

Life has been very good
often you put us in good mood
I and the others admire your attitude
in rendering services with gratitude
that made hard work become light
accomplishing our job with delight.

Mentor like you who is dedicated
anything you did even so complicated
made us your subordinates love our work
and we enjoyed doing it unplugging the cork
realizing that whatever difficulty we face
in this world we must continue the pace
letting no problems impede us in any case.

Marvin Brato Sr.

Contents

Foreword

If you're lucky enough, someone significant may cross your path at some point, leaving you puzzled as to why your lives have collided. They might have added tremendous value to your lives. You must be thinking, why should having a great mentor be important to you? Because mentorship is important. Which is why the author wrote the book *"Implementor: Every leader needs to know how to do an extraordinary transformation of people by bridging differences for better mentoring and creating value in other people's lives."* Because the benefits of engaging with individuals to construct adaptive, more personalised mentoring frameworks depending on mentees' aspirations and lifestyles are well-known to the author. His compassion, kindness, and interest in individuals and society at large are commendable qualities that promote the effectiveness of his one-on-one mentoring approach. In this book, the author not only offers mentoring guidance but also exposes the reader to some of his mentees who have excelled in their fields.

Just like strategy, writing a book takes deep contemplation to narrate a theory in a very lucid manner. Hence, the author could establish his thought process for readers. This book is an integrated learning vehicle for all working professionals, irrespective of their role in an organization, to understand the deeper meaning of mentorship, methods to build mentoring capabilities and sharpen their mentoring skills for those who are working in any capacity in any organization.

In this book, the author chose to look at multiple facets of mentorship and how one can sharpen their mentorship prowess in this volatile, uncertain, complex market. The author takes a look at reverse mentoring and how this change in the typical mentor-mentee relationship can empower and build invaluable skills in younger employees. The author made this choice because his research indicates that leaders are hungry to know about unique mentoring qualities that are necessary to fulfil the expectations of an individual in an organization. Indeed, his diverse life experiences serve as a spark for his unique approach, which goes beyond the conventional one-size-fits-all concept.

Besides, the author has held industrial experience for more than two decades and has proved to be a successful HR-L&D and leadership practitioner professionally as well as an academic who very well understands teaching and research pedagogy. One of the best things about the author is that he is able to apply concepts literally and takes a practical view of things rather than simply incorporating models without any rational implication.

So, happy reading and learning to all readers.

Preface

"A mentor is someone who sees more talent and ability within you, than you see in yourself, and helps bring it out of you." - *Bob Proctor*

According to the dictionary, *"implementor"* means someone or something that puts a decision, plan, agreement, etc. into effect. The author has laid out the core of what it means to be an **I-M-P-L-E-M-E-N-T-O-R** in a convenient acronym, with each letter outlining a key aspect of defining mentorship and the chapters of this book and bringing it to fruition.

I- Introduction (understanding mentorship)
M- Mentoring qualities, characters, and skills
P- Pitfalls in mentoring
L- Leading your organization to success
E- Expectations building in mentorship
M- Mentoring Relationship building
E- Effective goals setting in mentorship
N- Newer generation newer approaches
T- Technological advancement in mentorship
O- Organizational capability building
R- Reverese mentroship a silver bullet

You chose this book because mentoring is something you're passionate about. You enjoy assisting or guiding others and sharing your knowledge with individuals who are important to you. Each of us can name at least one person who had a significant and positive impact on our lives. They swayed our opinions and impacted our decisions. Our mentors are the wiser, more experienced people in our lives who have gently nudged and directed us along the path to keep us on track. This book will show you how a small group of us managed to get the attention and access of talented, compassionate people. Whatever your reasons for reading this book, I'm glad you're doing it. We hear stories about great entrepreneurs who credit their success to getting the correct advice from the right people at the right moment. It's like having someone keep an eye on you, and that's a priceless benefit. Access to exceptional mentors is described as one of the major value propositions for entrepreneurs by leading entrepreneur networks such as Y-Combinator, 500 Startups, Alchemist, Startups.co, Founder Institute, Boot Up World, and Unreasonable Institute, to mention a few.

In this VUCA world, organizations are becoming leaner, flatter, and even meaner. Many people have become millionaires as a result of the dot.com boom and stock market gains. Many companies today wish to have a mentorship programmeme as a visible demonstration of their concern and care for their employees. The greater cost-effectiveness of enabling people to deliver results will gratify decision makers, who will support the process in both good and bad times. Mentoring procedures are currently primarily driven by recruitment, retention, and the creation of a more diverse workforce. I believe that mentoring will become ingrained in the culture of every Organization. New or existing employees, regardless of their professional level, will have a choice of mentors to assist them in quickly integrating into the workplace and learning the values, communication channels, and how things function. The mentoring process will be a choice-based intervention.

In this book, I'd like to share with you everything I've learned over the previous 25 years about how to make mentoring work. While reading, I noticed several examples of how people are applying the ideas and tactics given in this book when reading articles. Those examples demonstrate that it is more than just magic! My own experience with fast promotion processes in three large Organizations continues to serve as the inspiration for my design of guided mentoring. According to the Mahabharata, one of Hinduism's sacred texts, Arjuna was mentored by Krishna. He took his counsel and acted on it, which led to his eventual success. From the epic Mahabharata, I learned the value of having a mentor. To succeed, choose the proper mentor and listen to what he has to offer.

The Secret of Success, is of no secret. All you need is to have a mentor to be Successful!

A mentor can help you get started on your goals and assist you in setting the right ones for your life. Your mentor gives you the best billion-dollar advice and leads you down the path to success. The nicest aspect is that you learn from his mistakes. A mentor's role in safeguarding and nourishing his mentee's growth path is crucial, as he has much superior vision and foresight to determine the long-term impact of today's actions. Krishna shielded his mentee from danger and damage numerous times, either through smart advice or by physically removing him from the danger's path. Mentors, or Gurus, as they were known back then, have existed since the periods of Vishnupuran, Ramayana, and Mahabharata. These Gurus usually advised and guided the kings in all matters spiritual and kingship so that the kingdom's people were happy and peace and prosperity could be achieved. Socrates, the Greek philosopher, might have been found strolling the streets of Athens two and a half millennia ago, mingling with and confronting his fellow citizens. One of those whom he mentored was Plato. Despite the fact that the two men never met, Mandela credits Gandhi with inspiring his leadership.

Marlon Brando, a two-time Oscar winner for Best Actor who was once dubbed the "Actor of the Century" by Time Magazine, was one of Adler's classmates and mentees. Marlon Brando was mentored by Stella Adler. Musicians Ray Charles was a mentor to Quincy Jones, the great musician. In so many respects, it's a different planet. Two noteworthy examples are Mark Zuckerberg and Steve Jobs. Maya Angelou, the acclaimed author and poet, is Oprah Winfrey's mentor. Ray Charles, a musician, was a mentor to Quincy Jones, a notable musician. Richard Branson, co-founder of the Virgin Group, has written numerous pieces about the impact mentors have had on his professional achievement. Alexander the Great regarded Aristotle as his master in Greek history. Many figures in Indian history were trained by their mentors, such as Chandragupta Maurya by Kautilya, Swami Vivekananda by Ramakrishna Paramahamsa, and Pandit Nehru by Mahatma Gandhi, to name a few. Mentorship was used to pass down ancient knowledge and talents from one generation to the next. Even Richard Branson and Howard Schultz, the CEO of Starbucks, confess "they don't know everything, as I learned." When they're stuck, they seek out the advice of others to help them move forward more quickly. Choosing a mentor is a process that takes time. Smart entrepreneurs continue to seek advice, education, and guidance from experts throughout their lives. A mentor can make a significant difference in your professional and personal life. Bring reasonable expectations for the role and a desire to work hard for the partnership. Although the positive impact of a mentor's guidance and wisdom may not be felt for several years, you will eventually recognise it and go on to become a mentor to others. Mother Teresa dedicated her life to serving others and was regarded as one of the most noble individuals of the twentieth century, running orphanages, AIDS hospices, and other charitable Organizations all over the world. She lived a wonderful and acclaimed life, but without her mentor, Father Michael van der Peet, she might not have accomplished as much as she did. Tendulkar is said to have coached Sehwag, teaching him the value of focusing on becoming the best Sehwag he can be rather than trying to emulate Tendulkar. At the legal firm where they both worked as summer associates, Michelle Robinson (now known as Michelle Obama) was designated as Barack's mentor. As evidenced by these examples, mentoring has clearly stood the test of time as one of the techniques utilised by champions to achieve their destiny's destination.

I think back on my mentor. He was one of the first individuals to tell me that I didn't have to apologise for desiring a sense of balance in my life. We've been in touch, and he continues to I think back on my mentor. He was one of the first individuals to tell me that I didn't have to apologise for desiring a sense of balance in my life. We've been in touch, and he continues to assist me in calibrating and prioritising some important aspects of my life. He showed me how to break down the problems at hand, build effective slides, and present ideas to clients. What I really appreciated was how he did it in such an objective way. He placed my excitement and needs above the office's interests. Hence, our mentors are the ones that light the fire in our hearts when it comes to business. We all need mentors. They motivate us, assist us in difficult situations, and direct our paths.

You will agree that, by any measure, the corporate climate is unpredictable. What would your organization's scorecard look like if you scored yourselves as employers who empower your people holistically to be more effective in their jobs? Internal and external dynamics play a role in the constantly shifting path that enterprises must take on a daily basis. Are we asking ourselves this as people leaders before sketching up development programmes and mapping them to organisational needs? Some of the more forward-thinking ones devised a "mentor-mentee" programme for mid-level managers that extends beyond the original hiring process and serves as a formative role for them, with the goal of strengthening their competencies and preparing them for more senior responsibilities. By utilising technology, you can make the most of accessible mentorship relationships. When looking at mentor-mentee relationships, it's important to remember that the mentor-mentee connection is a two-way street. By looking beyond your organization and engaging with your professional network, you may cast a broad net for mentorship possibilities.

A mentoring culture allows firms to bring on board not only profitable but also fascinating ideas, boosting their innovation quotient and giving them a competitive advantage. This, in my opinion, is the one that provides the most bang for the buck, given that it is not something that the organisation has mandated as a deliverable and is based on a relationship. When it comes to business, your mentors are the ones that kindle the fire in your hearts. They inspire you, help you through difficult times, and direct your paths.

Many of the world's most well-known entrepreneurs have mentors, as you may know. They recognise that success is not a one-person show, and that mentors can assist them in keeping their company current and inventive. With so many of the world's most notable executives going on record to thank a mentor for part of their success, the relationship between a mentor and a mentee can be the most influential in business. Mentorship is one of the most underappreciated and underutilised talent management techniques. Mentorship has the potential to help individuals for a lifetime.

If you're in charge of a team in today's workplace, you're probably dealing with numerous generations—often up to four! As the workplace experiences a significant demographic shift, multigenerational management has become a hot issue in recent months.Despite the fact that different generations have had diverse life experiences, we all have more in common than we know.Most of us would benefit from having a mentor who could assist us at work and serve as a guide and sounding board as we progress in our careers. Mentorship is a natural action in which we all participate without even realising it. Whether you want to be mentored to acquire a new skill, advance in your careers, or gain a new perspective, you all want to improve yourselves. Learning from those who have gone before you is an excellent way to avoid making costly mistakes. Mentorship teaches mentors a lot about themselves, and they can use what they've learned to tackle their own difficulties and challenges in new and better ways. Which is why mentorship has been regarded as a crucial part in the success of many of the world's most renowned people, including Bill Gates and Bill Clinton. Traditional mentoring methods have failed to keep up with advances in today's corporate environment, despite the clear benefits of mentoring. As a result, promote and sustain mentoring at your company by emphasising its importance and stressing how connections serve as a catalyst for transformation for both mentors and mentees. Also, create formal mentorship programmes that allow workers to participate in personal and professional growth that is directed by the organization's structure. Let's be open to forming a mentorship connection with someone who is different from us in terms of race, gender, or age—it can help us get new ideas and views on others' work experiences.

Acknowledgements

At the outset, I will thank my family for supporting me throughout the journey of writing my book and encouraging me to live my dreams; my son has always been instrumental in giving his inspiration to complete the writing of this book. Lastly, I would like to thank all the people with whom I have been associated. You gave me power. Finally, thank you all for gifting your time to read this book. I also would like to thank Notion Press Publication for publishing my book.

CHAPTER ONE

INTRODUCTION

"A mentor is someone who allows you to see the hope inside yourself."
-Oprah Winfrey

The word "mentor" originally appeared in ancient Greek literature, in Homer's epic "The Odyssey," in which Odysseus spent 20 years away from home battling and wandering. During that period, Telemachus, the son he had abandoned as a baby, grew up under the watchful eye of Mentor, an old trusted friend. When the goddess Athena decided it was time to finish young Telemachus' education, she came to him disguised as Mentor, and the two of them set off to learn about his father. Since then, the character's name has become a slang phrase for trustworthy tutor. Mentors have existed since people first walked the world. If we didn't have mentors, we would have to learn everything from scratch every time we started a new activity. It's priceless to have someone who can extract years of hard-won knowledge in a week or two. So, what exactly do we mean when we say mentorship? A mentor, by definition, is a more experienced and knowledgeable person who instructs and guides the growth of a less experienced individual. We now use the term "mentor" to denote someone who has a constructive, guiding influence on another's life, but why do we need someone to assist us in improving our lives?

According to Wikipedia, *"mentorship is a relationship in which a more experienced or knowledgeable person helps to advise a less experienced or knowledgeable person."* Mentorship may take various forms, but it always boils down to building a mutually beneficial, supportive connection between two individuals who want to see one another thrive. At least once, I've had at least one individual hold me responsible for my professional growth goals throughout my whole career. They inspire me. They mentor me and share their knowledge and expertise with me.

Mentors shape the lives of their mentees by selflessly devoting themselves to guiding them down the right road.

Everything changes when the proper person appears. A wonderful mentor is at the heart of many successful stories. Even if someone claims to have created their own route, there's a good possibility that someone was there to guide them or give them sound counsel early on. Virendra Rathore, a well-known film and media industry talent mentor, was named the first recipient of a new category of prizes, Best Mentor – Film Academy, by the renowned Dadasaheb Phalke Film Foundation Awards. In the past, mentors from well-known film institutes were never recognised in this way. Rathore has over 5 million followers on YouTube and other social media sites. He was the first to start free video tutorials on YouTube for budding artists and was a pioneer in the concept of sharing work-related information about the film industry. Thus, it is not a surprise that Join Films is famous for backing talents without a Godfather in the film industry.

"The idea is that everyone should be able to not only chase their dreams but also get work in films without getting trapped in the web of fraudsters." -Virendra Rathore is a hindi film Producer and Director.

Mentoring is crucial for professional development and learning. 62.7% of professionals prefer to participate in an upskilling program that includes a mentor. A mentor is more than a confidante or teacher. They shape destinies by selflessly guiding their mentees down the right road. 87.9% of respondents believe that having access to a seasoned mentor may significantly improve their career. 79.4% believe that working with a mentor is one of the best ways to move to a new field. 41.9 percent of professionals said they needed a mentor to help them. Mentoring programs fill opportunity gap that keeps people from advancing within organizations or while changing jobs. Virtual mentoring programs can assist people all over the world to achieve their career goals. There is a pressing need to reassess how growth and development are viewed by everyone, from leaders to job seekers.

Mentorship at work can encourage employees to learn and improve by exposing them to new learning opportunities and providing assistance. Mentor-mentee relationships are frequently mutually developmental for both mentor and mentee. In the Ramayana, we learn about Hanuman, who was inspired to fly across the sea by Jambavant. In the Mahabharata, Krishna was Arjuna's instructor. Many figures in Indian history were trained by their mentors, such as Chandragupta Maurya by Kautilya, Swami Vivekananda by Ramakrishna Paramahamsa, and Pandit Nehru by Mahatma Gandhi, to name a few. Mentorship was used to pass down ancient knowledge and talents from one generation to the next. Successful mentoring can be found in herbal medicine, yoga, classical music, dance, folk art, and literature.

Excellent mentors offer emotional support in the form of counselling, validation, and encouragement. For example, when singer Justin Bieber was first starting out, Usher, a well-known artist, took him under his wing and told him he believed in him. Speaking words of opportunity and optimism to your mentee may be really effective. Third, outstanding mentors act as good role models for their students. Remember that your proteges are always observing and learning from you. Consider what you want your proteges to learn from you the most. Finally, exceptional mentors understand that the most effective mentoring relationships are two-way streets. Throughout history, famous people have been guided by similarly important or influential others. History is replete with such examples: Elizabeth Taylor as Audrey Hepburn's mentee; Gandhiji as Gopala Krishna Gokhale's mentee; Gandhiji as a mentor to Nelson Mandela and Martin Luther King Jr. Thousands of instructors and students around the world, I'm sure, have personal experiences with her that far outnumber mine.

Who Needs Mentorship and Why?

To be successful and apply oneself in a world that is constantly changing, it is necessary to not only improve yourself and your unique abilities, but also to adjust to these changes. A mentor is a person who assists you in developing new abilities, making better decisions, and gaining new insights into your life & profession. Mentors provide guidance, advice, feedback, and support to mentees, acting as role models, teachers, counsellors, advisors, sponsors, advocates, and allies, depending on the mentee's individual aims and objectives. A mentor, in general, is an experienced and trusted expert who provides personalised direction and counsel to someone with less experience. The formal mentoring process includes creating precise goals and objectives and assisting the mentee in gaining information, developing abilities, and or changing attitudes with the assistance of the mentor. During this stage, the mentor serves as a learning intermediary, a sounding board, and occasionally an instructor or coach for the mentee. Preparation, bargaining, facilitating progress, and closing are the four stages of a successful mentoring relationship.

Fundamental Differences Between Coaching and Mentoring

Let's take a closer look at the distinctions. A mentor is someone with whom you have a long-term connection, whereas a coach is someone with whom you have a short-term relationship. It's more informal with a mentor since you're creating a trusted connection, but it's more regimented with a coach. A mentor takes a long-term, okay, larger picture of a person, whereas a coach takes a more short-term approach and focuses on a specific development need. A mentor will share their knowledge and expertise, and they will usually be a little more senior or experienced than you, but a coach does not need to have any prior experience in the field. They're on your side in this. As previously said, a mentor focuses on your overall professional and personal growth, whereas a coach, as previously said, focuses on immediate goals. In a recent poll, employees were asked what they would change about their boss. The second most frequent response was for their manager to resign.

I'm here to ensure that none of your staff are thinking the same thing. You all want your employees to be able to work with exceptional leaders. You also know that exceptional leaders aren't necessarily born with such qualities. Most managers require assistance in becoming what I refer to as a magnetic leader. These are the types of leaders that have an easy time attracting and retaining talent.

Coaching is aimed at achieving specific objectives (for example, an increase in employee management; speech structuring; strategic thinking development). To achieve these objectives, a professional "coach" is necessary; someone who understands and can manage such objectives. To put it another way, the first goal is to clearly identify the task and successfully complete it.

The goal of coaching is to promote personal efficiency and professional development. These words refer to either improving existing knowledge or acquiring new ones. The process might be regarded as complete after the trainee has acquired appropriate knowledge. Because they provide feedback on their employee's results and missing skills, current supervisors at work assume a dominant role in the trainee's coaching process. This data is used to construct the interactions. While the coaching process can be considered accomplished after a few sessions, due to the unique nature of mentoring, it can take up to a year. Coaching has a certain objective in mind and is working towards achieving it.

Mentorship, on the other hand, prioritises human relationships (for example, a "mentee" could have the desire to share his or her life or job challenges that prevent him from achieving success). Without a doubt, certain abilities and competences are required to establish trust relationships, which define more advanced strategies such as: life or career balance or harmony; self-confidence; self-perception; and the understanding that one's personal life influences one's work life.

Mentorship In An Organizational Context

Workplaces can be high-pressure environments. There are not only the usual deadlines and day-to-day chores that come with every employment, but there are also the social stresses that come with working in a group. Because they are coping with the added stress of preparing to take on more responsibility, business leaders often feel more pressure than their employees. Mistakes made at the top of the totem pole definitely have a greater impact on the company's health than those made at the bottom. Employees should be reminded that mentoring may take place informally and organically within established professional networks, and that it can be aided by attending networking events such as conferences, seminars, or webinars. For many in India, the recent shift to remote work has had a substantial impact on their career advancement and development prospects. There is a pressing need to reassess how growth and development are viewed by everyone, from leaders to job seekers. By filling important holes in the current labour market, virtual mentoring programs can assist people all over the world to achieve their career goals.

Understanding The Nitty-Gritty Of Mentorship

A specific length of time is required in order to get the most out of a mentoring session. This time is utilised to get to know each other's personalities and to create an environment where a "mentee" can feel comfortable sharing his personal and professional concerns with his mentor. Mentoring is geared toward lifelong learning, which can be applicable not only to the existing job, but to the future one as well. As a result, the mentor's ideas and learning methods bring a constant and universal development essence that is unattached to any specific location of self-realization. In mentoring, the supervisor does not affect the process, but he or she can and will provide recommendations to his or her employee. This method ensures that mentorship encounters are independent and has a favourable impact on the ultimate result. By acting as a confidant, a mentor can assist a future leader in dealing with all of this. A leader can go to his mentor with any of his business and personal issues. This can be extremely beneficial to his growth and productivity. It cannot be emphasised how valuable it is for a manager to have someone he can turn to for counsel who will not only listen but also empathise because they have been there before.

Tweet: " Usually, when entrtepreneurs are about to quit, it is just before a major breakthrough. So, keep going, don't stop. Also, select your founding team carefully. Be sure they are people that complement your skillset and have the right personality." -Sarika Batra Shoruner & Director of Meet the Drapers.

Do Mentors and Mentees Work Well Together?

There is a well-known anecdote about two renowned composers, Ludwig Van Beethoven and Wolfgang Amadeus Mozart, meeting in Vienna in 1787. Beethoven's hero and role model was Mozart. Beethoven is reported to have taken time off from his royal orchestra duties in Bonn to visit Vienna in order to meet Mozart and potentially study under him. When Beethoven arrived at Mozart's house, he was not greeted warmly. He was unwell and in the middle of working on a composition. Beethoven persevered, and Mozart requested him to play a piano piece. He instantly chose Mozart's Piano Concerto No. 24 in C Minor, only for the latter to interrupt him in the middle of the piece with an admonishment. Mozart requested that the younger maestro play something fresh rather than flattery. Beethoven is claimed to have performed the first bars of his inspiration for what would later become the "Tempest" sonata right away. A visibly ecstatic Mozart is reported to have dashed out of the chamber to summon his wife and children to hear a glistening Beethoven, proclaiming him to be someone the world should keep an eye on. Beethoven's family situation prevented him from continuing to study with Mozart for a longer period of time, but the adulation continued. Mozart was Beethoven's mentor, and he is reported to have corresponded with him. Mozart had been friends with and trained by the renowned composer Joseph Haydn, he must have been both a muse and a wonderful mentor. A mentor is more than a confidante or a teacher. In the best of situations, mentors shape destinies by selflessly guiding their mentees down the right road and providing them with opportunities to flourish. The accomplishment of a mentee is a shared victory for a mentor and a mentee, a manifestation of belief and proof of their trust in one another.

Bird's-Eye View On Mentorship

According to the survey, a staggering 87.9% of respondents believe that having access to a seasoned mentor may significantly improve their career success and trajectory, and 79.4% believe that working with a mentor is one of the best ways to move to a new field. Having access to an experienced mentor can assist professionals in identifying and bridging skill gaps as well as accelerating knowledge development in order to attain their career objectives. When asked about problems in their professional development, 41.9 percent of professionals said they needed a mentor to help them. The demand for mentor-led, career-focused partnerships is exactly what today's career-changers and job-seekers need, according to the Springboard mentoring study, as more individuals work from home amid the ongoing COVID-19 pandemic. Because of the pandemic, there is a greater need for people to seek mentoring while learning. While 69.4 percent of respondents believe that re-skilling is important for job advancement, 79 percent are willing to participate in a re-skilling program that provides them with one-on-one mentoring. Mentorship is critical to success, and it is also one of the most powerful areas that people confuse with teaching. A mentor is someone you may look up to for professional and personal advice at any moment in your life. They can help you succeed at work and in life. In today's competitive milieu, this is a less usual practise.

79% professionals prefer an up skilling program that gives them access to a mentor.

The survey's preliminary findings revealed that not every professional could tell the difference between teaching and mentoring. Mentoring and teaching are both vital, but when it comes to professional development and learning, the process is more crucial. According to the survey, 62.7 percent of professionals prefer to participate in an upskilling program that includes a mentor.

"The survey has brought to the fore many points. Firstly, intentional mentorship program have a definite impact on filling the opportunity gap that keeps people from advancing within organizations or while changing jobs. Secondly, there is a great potential in every professional looking to upskill – they just need to be directed and guided in the right manner. Our survey has shown us that, while content and certifica-tion are just the tip of the iceberg and can help a professional grow only to a certain extent whereas effective mentoring can do wonders by applying that knowledge at the right place, in the right manner." -Vivek Kumar, Managing Director, Springboard India.

Mentorship & The Startup World

In the startup world, a mentor is someone who has a track record of bringing ideas to fruition. A startup mentor has already made the journey and can give advice to a less experienced entrepreneur on what to expect along the route. Business mentorship is more than a one-way street; it is a mutually beneficial partnership. The person being mentored has access to someone with expertise and knowledge, while the mentor is able to form reliable business ties. Give yourself the best chance at success, no matter where you are on your business journey: locate a mentor to walk alongside you and share their advice and experience. You'll not only have a sympathetic ear to listen to your difficult problems, but you'll also have access to a larger pool of knowledge and skills to put your ideas into action. Sandeep Aggarwal, founder of Shopclues and Droom, says When he was in the U.S. contemplating becoming an entrepreneur in India, Narendra Bakshi, a successful entrepreneur and one of his associates in Silicon Valley, helped him decide when to take the plunge. He often asked him when he would be ready. Mr. Narendra Bakshi said, "When you stop asking that question?" Mr. Bakshi also urged Aggarwal to create a narrative around his path, such as embracing entrepreneurship on Father's Day to remind him to nurture his firm as if he were rearing a child. A skilled mentor can not only assist you in defining your company's value proposition but also guide you through the stages of establishment, consolidation, and expansion. With the proper mentor, you'll be able to find rapid solutions to the tougher challenges, saving you time, stress, and money. For example, when Mark Zuckerberg was starting Facebook, he was smart enough to know what he didn't know, which was being a CEO, so Zuckerberg wisely developed a mentoring relationship with Donald Graham, the CEO of the Washington Post. In both cases, Zuckerberg needed coaching on leading an organization, and in return, Zuckerberg reverse mentored Graham about social media. So what do great mentors actually do? First, they give task support. They provide task support through sponsorship, introductions, and critical feedback. For example, it's really interesting to know that Google co-founders Sergey Brin and Larry Page had the late, great Steve Jobs as their mentor. Mentorship has been regarded as a crucial part in the success of many of the world's most renowned people, including Bill Gates and Bill Clinton. Traditional mentoring methods have failed to keep up with advances in today's corporate environment, despite the clear benefits of mentoring. Mentoring programs predicated on length of service with a single organization no longer represent reality.

Summing Up

Great mentors understand that the most effective mentoring relationships are two-way streets. Gandhiji as a mentor to Nelson Mandela and Martin Luther King Jr. is one of the few examples of such a relationship. A mentor, in general, is an experienced and trusted expert who provides personalised direction and counsel to someone with less experience. The formal mentoring process includes creating precise goals and objectives and assisting the mentee in gaining information, developing abilities, and or changing attitudes. It's more informal with a mentor since you're creating a trusted connection, but it's more regimented with a coach. Business mentorship is more than a one-way street; it is a mutually beneficial partnership. With the proper mentor, you'll be able to find rapid solutions to the tougher challenges, saving you time and money. Virtual mentoring programmes can assist people all over the world to achieve their career goals. A specific length of time is required in order to get the most out of a mentoring session. Mentoring is geared toward lifelong learning, which can be applicable to the existing job as well as the future one.

CHAPTER TWO

MENTORING QUALITIES, CHARACTERS & SKILLS

"Mentoring is a brain to pick, an ear to listen, and a push into the right direction."

-John C. Crosby

Qualities Of A Good Mentor

Your mentor should, more often than not, have some form of relevant background, which may seem obvious. They should, however, be able to assist you in moving forward because they've been there, seen the landscape, and understand what it takes to succeed. You don't want someone who is rude and unconstructive in their criticism, who mistreats you or others close to you, and gives you a terrible reputation. For the relationship to be beneficial, a good mentor must be available to their mentee for a decent amount of time each day or week. Create a plan that works best for your mentor to demonstrate that you value their time and appreciate the effort they put into your development. Rather than aimlessly soliloquizing about their expertise, they prefer to see their mentee implement adjustments that have measurable outcomes.

If you're a mentor, make sure to put what you teach into practise.

- A good mentor must have a positive attitude and a willingness to help others grow.
- It necessitates an openness to consider and share one's own experiences, including failures.
- He must have a drive to grow and assist others.
- He must have the willingness and ability to devote significant time and effort to the mentoring relationship.
- He must have knowledge, competence, and or abilities in the current and relevant industry or organization.
- The finest mentors are experts in the field in which the mentee aspires to advance.
- He must have a willingness to share personal flaws and experiences.
- He should have a growth mindset and be willing to learn.
- Mentors who are curious learners have always been and will continue to be the best teachers.
- He must possess active listening skills, ask compelling, open-ended questions, self-reflection, provide feedback, and the ability to communicate tales that incorporate personal experiences, case examples, and honest insight. Unlike Alexa, who can perform a variety of chores for you, the mentor responds to your emotions in addition to pointing you in the right direction.
- The most crucial quality of a mentor is that he or she is available, approachable, and eager to listen, respond, and share.
- A mentor's ego, pride, and domineering behaviour might turn him or her into a tormentor! A mentor is similar to a gardener who cares for the plants, irrigates them, and feeds them with fresh ideas to help them flourish. In the mind of the mentee, the gardener likewise pulls out ignorance and uncertainty.
- A mentor who is willing to grow alongside you rather than assume a position of superiority is extremely useful because they take the time to thoughtfully investigate and answer any queries they don't know the solution to right away.

- Good mentors know how to deliver constructive feedback in a way that makes their mentee feel encouraged rather than despondent.
- Instead of showing you how to accomplish something, they'll describe how they tackle certain difficulties and circumstances. As the fable goes, they won't give you a fish; instead, they'll teach you how to fish.
- They shouldn't be someone who reluctantly shares information in exchange for a figurative payment, nor should they provide information in a vague, manipulative manner. Rather, they should be welcoming and enthusiastic about spreading the news.

Qualities Of A Good Mentee

- Consider utilizing self-disclosure with your mentor and giving them something personal about yourself that may reveal that you are not flawless.
- Furthermore, when your mentor reciprocates, keep this knowledge safe with your life.
- Effective mentees are self-assured. If you're worried about your lack of confidence, rest assured that many successful individuals battle with it.
- You don't have to be fully certain about everything in your life all of the time. After all, many of us seek out mentors to increase our self-esteem.
- Consider your strengths and increasing your knowledge of what you are excellent at as a strategy to raise your confidence.
- Effective mentees contribute value to the lives of their mentors. They might just be sharing a talent with their mentor that the mentor lacks.
- Bring a modest gift or token that you believe your mentor would appreciate. Support them on LinkedIn. Send them a message expressing your gratitude. It actually doesn't matter what you do, as long as you do something and do it on a regular basis.

- Convey your good vibes to your mentor. Stephanie Johnson's research reveals that energy and emotions are infectious. The energy test is one of my litmus tests for determining whether a mentoring relationship will survive.
- Remember that being a successful mentee does not require you to be flawless.
- One attribute that differentiates great mentors from good mentors is their ability to inspire their mentees to achieve greatness. By setting an example and supporting them in meeting further inspirational people and circumstances, you may guide your mentees along future paths that thrill and motivate them—even beyond their original dreams.
- Convey your good vibes to your mentor. Stephanie Johnson's research reveals that energy and emotions are infectious. The energy test is one of my litmus tests for determining whether a mentoring relationship will survive.

Characteristics Of An Excellent Mentors

- Knowledgeable
- Nonjudgmental
- Able to give constructive feedback
- Honest and candid
- Able to network and find resources
- Honest and candid
- Able to network and find resources
- Successful in career
- Willing/able to devote time to developing others
- Eager to learn
- Good listener/sounding board
- FlexibleValue diversity of perspectives

Characteristics of An Excellent Mentee

- Be efficient and systematic

- Personal commitment
- Be considerate to schedule meetings ahead of time, value your mentor's time
- Flexible
- Opneness & Open-mindedness
- Be trustworthy
- Be resourceful
- Initiator
- Be proactive, bring up relevant matters to discuss with your mentor
- Be realistic and learn from mistakes
- Be curious and engaged

"Nobody cares how much you know until they know how much you care." -Theodore Roosevelt

Mentorship Skills

Mentorship, as previously said, is a two-way street. This implies that, like the mentee, you should know what kind of relationship you want and what you want to get out of it. A mentor is a member of a network of assisting connections who offers task and emotional assistance as well as acts as a role model. The key to this concept, in my opinion, is that mentoring does not have to be a monogamous relationship. This should relieve some of your stress. It is not your obligation to meet your protege's requirements all of the time. Teach your mentee what you're good at and link them with additional resources. Mentors have the capacity to apply their experience, expertise, and viewpoints to another person's circumstance and provide guidance and direction without pushing an agenda. Mentors provide a perspective on the topic or decision that their mentees are facing without passing judgement or bias. In some circumstances, the problem is as easy as deciding how to manage career development; in others, it's as difficult as resolving a sensitive workplace conflict or making a critical strategic growth decision. A mentor can provide guidance for the rest of your life or just help you get through the next week. It's no surprise, therefore, that when individuals tell us about leaders who have made a significant impact on their lives, they commonly mention those who believe in them and inspire them to overcome their own self-doubts and discover their own greatest abilities. They talk of leaders that treat them in ways that boost their self-esteem, allowing them to do more than they first thought was possible.

Mentor's Self-Introspection

- How can you hone your skills in your field?
- Do you have any connections or knowledge gaps?
- How can taking on a mentorship role in your personal and professional life help you grow as a leader?

Setting expectations is the next logical step after determining what you want out of your mentorship relationship. Every relationship between a mentor and a mentee is unique. So, when you initially start out, talk to your mentee about expectations and whether you're ready to make that commitment.

- Is there a deadline for the mentoring to end?
- When should you meet, and why should you meet?
- What resources can the mentor supply so that the mentee may work independently?
- What criteria are used to assess success?
- What level of involvement should the mentor have?

The relationship between a mentor and a mentee is extremely intimate.

You may provide substandard advice without actually understanding a person, but you'll need to get to know your mentee on a personal level to stand out as an exceptional mentor. You probably already know the answers to some of the more career-related questions, such as their working style, dream job, current employment aspirations, and so on. But what about the substance that causes them to exist?Getting to know your mentee on a deeper level will aid in the development of a solid connection as well as a better understanding of who they are as people and how they interact with others.You must continue to create trust in order to maintain a safe atmosphere in which your mentee may discuss their worries and issues.

When you're mentoring someone, you could feel obligated to provide immediate advice. However, not all input is beneficial, and recognizing the difference is crucial. Whether you recognize it or not, biases impair our judgement. While you can attempt to identify and deconstruct them, some are so deeply embedded that they emerge without our knowledge. Breakthrough common assumptions with your mentee by asking questions and delving further to tackle this issue. This is especially true if you're mentoring someone who is just starting out in their career. Spend time asking questions that pull out the crucial aspects of their situation rather than telling a narrative about a time you experienced communication challenges with management. One of the most valuable gifts a mentor can provide is the willingness to share your own errors and disappointments. It not only provides useful information for problem-solving, but it also helps to create trust and deepen relationships. You're also developing your mentee's confidence and keeping them motivated when you take the time to acknowledge and even praise their victories and achievements. Many mentoring discussions centre on the unpleasant because people typically seek or rely on a mentor to help them deal with difficult situations.Great mentors seek out and even create opportunities to assist their mentees in achieving their objectives. It might be anything from putting them in touch with someone who has worked in their ideal career to proposing a conference they would enjoy. Take notice of your mentee's areas of interest and be on the lookout for new chances.

Expectations From A Skillful Mentor

- An excellent mentor is genuinely interested in assisting someone else without expecting anything in return. Mentorship is something that good people do because they sincerely want to see others succeed.

- The willingness and capacity to devote significant time and effort to the mentoring relationship. Mentorship requires time, not just good intentions.
- The finest mentors are experts in the field in which the mentee aspires to advance. They possess current and relevant knowledge, experience, and or abilities in the industry or organization.
- A willingness to discuss personal failures and experiences. Mentors must share both their *"how I did it well"* and *"how I did it poorly"* tales with their students. Both events mentors provide excellent learning opportunities.
- Avoid a deficit attitude that is unsupportive of what this new faculty member has to give. Find out what your mentee is good at, what they are enthusiastic about, and what they are working on.
- Address the given needs to the best of your ability. Only provide more when it is necessary. Don't judge, save, or condemn. Don't spread unfavourable information about the college or its personnel. Assist the mentee by acting as a learning broker and providing a sounding board for concerns concerning the mentee's professional goals and development.
- A mentor who is willing to grow alongside you rather than assume a position of superiority is extremely useful because they take the time to thoughtfully investigate and answer any queries they don't know the solution to right away.
- Good mentors know how to deliver constructive feedback in a way that makes their mentee feel encouraged rather than despondent. Instead of showing you how to accomplish something, they'll describe how they tackle certain difficulties and circumstances.
- The finest instructors have always been and will continue to be those who are interested learners. Would you want to be advised by someone whose mind is closed because he knows everything

or someone whose mind is open because she is always seeking to expand her knowledge?

- Give feedback or suggestions cautiously and only when requested explicitly. Recognize that your mentee may not comply. Suggest a second or third person's perspective as well, to assist your mentee in expanding his or her network.
- Respect your mentee's privacy—don't spread information that was intended to be shared between the two of you mandated reporter issues aside, of course.
- You should have a personal vision, clear goals, and a firm grasp of current realities. As a mentor, be clear about your mentees' hopes, desires, and work-life goals as a mentor, and communicate with them about them. They'll be interested in learning about your current reality, including your perceptions of your own strengths and limitations, as well as the current reality of situations inside your firm, and they'll need help recognizing their own.
- You should listen much more than you speak.
- Mentors that are effective are also willing and capable of shielding their mentees from disasters. One of your tasks as a mentor is to prevent your mentees from making costly mistakes while they learn to take appropriate risks. Managing risks is a subcategory of the previously described basic skill of creating trust.
- Avoid a deficit attitude that is unsupportive of what this new faculty member has to give. Find out what your mentee is good at, what they are enthusiastic about, and what they are working on.
- Your mentees are likely to face commercial and professional risks, which are potentially dangerous situations in which they might make huge errors and jeopardise their jobs, careers, or organisations.
- In addition to regular and honest positive feedback, effective mentors should be willing and capable of providing corrective criticism to their mentees.When you notice your mentees

making mistakes or performing in less-than-ideal ways, you should be open and honest with them, telling them what you observe and providing some solutions.

- Address the given needs to the best of your ability. Only provide more when it is necessary. Don't judge, save, or condemn. Don't spread unfavourable information about the college or its personnel. Assist the mentee by acting as a learning broker and providing a sounding board for concerns concerning the mentee's professional goals and development.
- Give feedback or suggestions cautiously and only when requested explicitly. Recognize that your mentee may not comply. Suggest a second or third person's perspective as well, to assist your mentee in expanding his or her network.
- Respect your mentee's privacy—don't spread information that was intended to be shared between the two of you (mandated reporter issues aside, of course.)
- Introduce your mentee to college, show your mentee around campus, and assist your mentee with critical deadlines like flex and co-curricular.
- Be a catalyst for the mentee's network development. Indicate who else he or she could reach out to and interact with.
- Be open about any little issues you have with the mentorship relationship. If things are just not functioning, accept the reality and implement a "no blame" separation policy if necessary.
- Be considerate of your mentee's time. Schedule as much as possible around her or his requirements, and let go of notions of how frequently you "should" meet. When meeting with your mentee, try to eliminate distractions like phones and knocks on the door.
- Be a catalyst for the mentee's network development. Indicate who else he or she could reach out to and interact with.
- Be open about any little issues you have with the mentorship relationship. If things are just not functioning, accept the reality and implement a "no blame" separation policy if necessary.

- Be considerate of your mentee's time. Schedule as much as possible around her or his requirements, and let go of notions of how frequently you "should" meet. When meeting with your mentee, try to eliminate distractions like phones and knocks on the door.
- Ability to mentor others. Active listening, asking compelling, open-ended questions, self-reflection, offering feedback, and the ability to communicate tales that incorporate personal experiences, case examples, and honest insight are all very real talents.
- Mentorship will fail if there is no commitment. We've seen firms pick managers and leaders at random for mentoring junior employees without even asking them if they wanted to coach in the first place. Many leaders, on the other hand, enjoy being labelled as mentors and want to mentor someone but are unsure of what it implies. In both circumstances, the mentorship was a failure. One of the attributes of a mentor, according to Mary Abbajay, is "the willingness and capacity to devote substantial time and effort to the mentoring connection." Mentorship requires time, not just good intentions.
- A good mentoring relationship necessitates a high level of dedication. For the mentoring process to work, both mentors and mentees need to believe in it. When a mentee enrols in a mentoring program, he or she is committing to unlearning and learning. The mentor's devotion will open up a world of change and transformation possibilities.
- The mentor may always ask the mentee a lot of questions to assist them in digging deeper. Listening is an art, and it requires fortitude and discipline to educate the mind to hear what the mentee is trying to say. By doing so, the mentor is empowering the mentee.
- It doesn't matter how much you know unless it matters how much you care. Roosevelt, Theodore This quote is the cornerstone of my mentorship program. To see true change, mentors must sincerely care about their mentees. A mentor

must have a high level of emotional intelligence to actually care.

- Mentors must have strong emotional intelligence in order to provide genuine care to their mentees while they work to solve challenges and advance. Mentors don't function on the basis of inciting fear; rather, they operate on the basis of caring.
- Mentors must be cautious about the words they use with their mentees. It has the potential to either strengthen or weaken the mentee. Mentors are being watched by their mentees as they come and go. Everything sends a signal to the mentee: the words uttered, the body language portrayed, the expressions.
- A good mentor must have a positive attitude and a willingness to help others grow. It necessitates an openness to consider and share one's own experiences, including failures. Mentors who can "speak the talk" and "walk the walk" are essential.
- A drive to grow and assist others. The willingness and ability to devote significant time and effort to the mentoring relationship.
- knowledge, competence, and or abilities in the current and relevant industry or organization. The finest mentors are experts in the field in which the mentee aspires to advance. A willingness to share personal flaws and experiences.A growth mindset and a willingness to learn.
- Unlike Alexa, who can perform a variety of chores for you, the mentor responds to your emotions in addition to pointing you in the right direction.
- The most crucial quality of a mentor is that he or she is available, approachable, and eager to listen, respond, and share.
- A mentor's ego, pride, and domineering behaviour might turn him or her into a tormentor!
- A mentor is similar to a gardener who cares for the plants, irrigates them, and feeds them with fresh ideas to help them flourish. In the mind of the mentee, the gardener likewise pulls out ignorance and uncertainty.
- Your mentor should, more often than not, have some form of relevant background, which may seem obvious. They should, however, be able to assist you in moving forward because

they've been there, seen the landscape, and understand what it takes to succeed.

- Use every chance to speak effectively to touch people's lives and bring about positive change. One cannot be nasty to one's teammates while being a wonderful mentor to another. The maturity of a mentor is determined by how well they communicate and improve relationships while addressing obstacles and solving problems.
- Respect is necessary to ensure your mentor's legitimacy on the subject or issue. There are many people who are eager to share their thoughts on what you should or should not do.
- Ideally, a mentor should be able to explain how the organization is structured; be someone who is respected as an experienced and successful professional in the organization; support the organization's mission, vision, and goals; stay accessible, communicative, and engaged throughout the duration of the program; offer encouragement through genuine positive reinforcement; be a positive role model; and share *"lessons learned"* from their own experiences.
- A mentor is a member of a network of assisting connections who offers task and emotional assistance as well as acts as a role model. The key to this concept, in my opinion, is that mentoring does not have to be a monogamous relationship. This should relieve some of your stress. It is not your obligation to meet your mentees requirements all of the time. Teach your mentee what you're good at and link them with additional resources.

"Assisting mentees in stepping out onto the branch and then flying when ready"

Expectations From An Effective Mentee

- Being an effective mentee takes a significant amount of work. In the spirit of professional self-reliance, you should be very active in seeking out and negotiating with numerous mentors who can help you achieve your goals.

- You must understand the acquisition process since competent mentors now have a huge pool of potential mentees to pick from.
- You will be able to identify a desired pool of people who could be able to mentor you after actively seeking out numerous mentors.
- Typically, your mentors expect you to be a *"fast learner."* You should make every effort to learn everything you can as rapidly as possible, both directly and indirectly.
- Convey your unique needs and goals to prospective mentors. In addition, set objectives, expectations, the length of your mentoring relationship, confidentiality, feedback systems, and meeting times with your mentors.
- You must incorporate new ideas you learn into your own conceptual framework.
- When you listen carefully, you demonstrate to your mentors that you have heard and grasped their concerns. People come to trust you as a result of feeling accepted by you.
- Keep any agreements made with your mentors; complete agreed-upon activities on time; test out their ideas and report back the results; explain ahead of time if you want to alter or break an agreement; and continue with difficult jobs even when discouraged.
- Remember, mentors enjoy working with mentees who learn quickly and pay attention to instructions.
- You must attentively watch and learn indirectly from your mentors' and others' modelled behaviours; read resources both those supplied by your mentors and materials you seek relating to your growth areas.
- You should know when to take the initiative and when not to, and ask the proper questions to clarify and learn more as a good mentee.
- To get through this journey, you'll need to be able to describe the general process of mentoring—how it works and why it's effective; communicate with each of your mentors about issues between you, goals to achieve, satisfaction with meeting

schedules, and so on.

- Mentees are encouraged to manage connections and take initiative under the most current mentoring approach. In any event, they'll be looking to you to take the initiative. They'll notice the things you do on your own to improve.
- It's up to you to keep the ties under control, even if your mentors want to take the lead. This is your development, and you must take responsibility for both the process and the outcomes.
- Despite this new trend, some mentors may attempt to take the initiative and expect you to follow. Others will turn to you to take the lead right away.
- Most mentors will expect you to follow them at times, particularly if your actions have the potential to harm them.
- You can assess the current status of your mentoring partnerships and decide where to go next with them; plan for the end of your mentoring relationships.

These days, it's a mentor's market. Mentees who fail to complete tasks and fulfil commitments are regularly replaced by those who do. Phillips-Jones conducted an informal poll of mentors and discovered that many were dissatisfied with mentees who did not follow through on agreed-upon responsibilities. Some mentors have even refused to take on new mentoring assignments. They came to the conclusion that they put more effort into the lives of their mentees than the mentees did into their own!

In an interview with USA Today, Sathya Nadella thinks "it's vital for leaders not to frighten people out, but to give them cover to fix the underlying problem." Nadella adds, "It's difficult or impossible to truly generate any innovation if people are acting out of fear."

Effectiveness Of Mentoring

Is mentoring still appropriate in today's hectic world? Is mentoring really effective? Is it true that mentoring is a complete waste of time? More than 70% of Fortune 500 businesses, according to the Association for Talent Development, a Virginia-based nonprofit focusing on workplace learning and professional development, have some form of mentoring program. So it's working, but how many people have fully realised the benefits of true mentoring? This brings us to the following question: what constitutes real mentoring? The following are some golden rules I use as a mentor to set the groundwork for a good mentoring process.

Mentorship is a fantastic way to grow and alter people's lives. *"The averageThe mentor tells, the competent mentor explains, the outstanding mentor displays, and the finest mentors inspire, "says Lucia Ballas Tryanor.*

Unfortunately, for many firms, mentoring programs have become a band-aid, minimising the significant impact that a proper mentoring program may have. Not every leader makes a good mentor. On the other hand, every excellent mentor is a capable leader. A mentoring process is fundamentally different from a therapy session in which a counsellor listens to the patient's situation and offers guidance and solutions.Mentors are typically in a position to elevate their mentees' status. This means opening the right doors for them, allowing them to meet new people and demonstrate their ability to a wide range of individuals. According to a study, mentors who advocate for their mentees in this way are more likely to have their work approved. According to Phillips-Jones' research, the most beneficial mentoring ability is expressing encouragement. This entails recognising and complimenting your mentoring partners in a genuine, positive manner. According to mentors and mentees in interviews, positive verbal reinforcement, or praise, was unusual and even openly rejected in many Fortune 500 companies. Most, on the other hand, stated they appreciated being recognised for their achievements and abilities, as well as receiving positive feedback, as long as it was genuine and not excessive.

Summing Up

Mentorship, as previously said, is a two-way street. You should know what kind of relationship you want and what you want to get out of it. A mentor can provide guidance for the rest of your life or just help you get through the next week. You need to get to know your mentee on a personal level to stand out as an exceptional mentor. Not all input is beneficial, and recognising the difference is crucial. As a great mentor, ask questions that pull out crucial aspects of their situation rather than tell a narrative. Also, take notice of your mentee's areas of interest and be on the lookout for new chances. Since, you're also developing your mentees' confidence and keeping them motivated when you acknowledge and praise their victories.

CHAPTER THREE

PITFALLS IN MENTORSHIP

"The delicate balance of mentoring somene is not creating them in your own image, but giving them the opportunity to create themselves."

-Steven Spielberg

Mentorship is the skill of unlocking potential in others, the capacity to identify a talent in them that others do not, and the ability to open doors of opportunity that might otherwise be closed. A mentorship program may be a truly gratifying experience with a clear knowledge of the intended objectives and a solid commitment from both sides. Of course, in order to mentor others, you must first achieve a particular degree of professional status, possess a specific level of competence, and have a demonstrated track record. Yet, in order to maintain that imagined position of relative authority, you may unintentionally slip into the crippling errors of mentorship. In order for a mentoring relationship to be productive, both sides must put in effort, with the mentee contributing somewhat more. It's time to talk to your mentee if he or she appears disengaged, lacking drive and or commitment. Understanding the underlying cause and or rationale for your disinterest is critical to resolving the problem before the connection becomes completely unproductive. The most effective mentoring relationships are those that develop naturally. Look for people with whom you share a natural bond. It shouldn't come across as forced. The better you know someone, and the better they know you, the more likely you are to receive actionable, individualized counsel.

A mentor once told me that the purpose and goal of leadership is to develop more leaders, not just followers, and to assist others in becoming greater leaders than you found them.

The genuinely outstanding mentors will be awestruck by how their mentees go about accomplishing what they do, and they will use the best of their mentees' talents to not only improve their skills and abilities, but also adapt them to their own lives."Leaders become great not because of their power but because of their ability to empower others." -John Maxwell

Flipside Of Mentorship

- Everyone tells you that they want you to be a great leader, that you can achieve anything if you put your mind to it, and that you can accomplish anything if you put your mind to it. One problem for many is when the individual you empower begins to show critical symptoms of achieving what you couldn't, of outperforming your outcomes. Then some you may perceive them as a threat as you begin to limit their prospects or take control of the situation so that you are still regarded as a leader.
- Many people place a high value on mentoring, which is a power-laden relationship that includes the transmission of information and skills. On the other hand, genuinely outstanding mentors understand that their mentees will teach them as much as they will educate them. It will astound even the most extraordinary mentors.
- Motivating mentors is one of the most difficult issues that workplace mentoring programs face. It might be tough to persuade competent and committed mentors to join your program. However, it does not have to be impossible. Begin by emphasising the program's benefits for mentors, such as improved abilities, the chance to assist others, and the opportunity to learn and grow themselves.

- There is a considerable possibility for one or both partners to grow dependent on the other in any supportive relationship, whether it be leading, managing, training, coaching, or mentoring.
- A mentee may assume that their mentor is uninterested in their professional development. The mentee's dissatisfaction and lack of direction might stymie his or her progress toward independence. Because of the power imbalance between mentor and mentee, resolving this issue while maintaining a productive and pleasant relationship is tough.
- To begin with, be conscious of your own bias. Many of you who want to advance your professions, as well as any firm that wants to develop a culture of diversity and inclusiveness, may face a significant obstacle in a society where people in positions of power and authority have traditionally appeared male and pale.
- Taking responsibility for the mentee is denying the mentee's ownership. That is to say, people-pleasing takes precedence over people-helping.
- Over-formalizing mentorship is the possible stumbling point. When companies recognise the importance of mentoring, they frequently establish official mentorship programs to facilitate interaction. While such efforts are unquestionably noble, one potential drawback is the excessive formality that they may introduce into this sort of partnership.
- People at the start of their careers have a tough time saying "no." Juniors who have several mentors or supervisors may feel overburdened with job obligations. Their workloads might become oppressive and a danger to their professional progress since they lack the knowledge to know how to prioritise these demands.
- A mentor may assume that his or her mentee lacks the passion and dedication necessary to create a successful career. This is a challenging circumstance for both the mentor and the mentee, since the mentee has a genuine risk of failing, and the mentor may think that he or she has squandered a lot of precious time

working with the mentee.

- For whatever reason, the mentee is unable to grasp and implement the mentor's vital advice. It's preferable if both parties agree to leave the relationship on a nice note and wish each other well in their future pursuits in these scenarios.
- Employee involvement may be made mandatory in some firms. Making the mentorship program mandatory, however, may elicit unfavourable reactions from potential participants, who may perceive it as a punishment or yet another company duty they don't have time for.
- Not every senior executive is suited to be a mentor to his or her subordinates. Mentors must be willing to devote a considerable amount of time and effort to the program, as well as possess the necessary abilities and insights to impart to their mentee.
- You can't understand what's being said because you don't understand what's being said. Many people mistake mentoring for a science in which mentors download material to their mentees and give unwanted advice in order for the mentee to pursue a specific path.
- Many mentors consider themselves to be the defenders of the mistake zone. They concentrate on what could be done better, how things should be done, and best practises that have been documented. It's the same as giving a sick individual a medication or an injection.
- You want to produce leaders who are carbon copies of yourself. When leaders set out to develop leaders who are split images of themselves, it's a recipe for disaster. You want to be a guide for people who want to be like you. Make the same judgments, think in the same way, and dress in the same way.
- It is unavoidable for mentees who have many mentors and advisers to get inconsistent advice on research or teaching plans, manuscript writing, and other elements of their professional development.
- Personal differences or clashing personalities might still cause a mismatch to emerge. Mentors are in a Goldilocks economic

scenario when it comes to delivering guidance.

- Perhaps the most significant impediment to effective mentoring is a lack of time. The mentor/mentee relationship might be harmed by missing scheduled visits or failing to show up due to other urgent obligations.

Actionable For Mentees

- It might be difficult to take harsh criticism, especially if you don't agree with it. However, keep an open mind. If you keep getting the same feedback, you should Pay attention to it.
- Based on their personal experiences, every mentor has a bias of some sort. Before acting on their advice, be sure you understand it and that it resonates with you.
- When you receive conflicting advice, consider what you want to do. Seek the advice of your friends. Speak with your coworkers and other members of your mentor team. Everyone has been in this scenario before, so people will be understanding while you figure out how to deal with it.
- Mentors can assist you with several parts of your job. Some may be excellent at guiding you through your career, while others may excel at dealing with challenging circumstances, and yet others may provide excellent direction or presentation skills. As a result, be certain that your mentors don't all fit the same mould.
- Co-create the agenda with your mentors, collecting their opinion first and only adding your ideas if you truly believe they would benefit. Also, always request permission at each step of the talk and before diving deeper into any aspect of it.
- It's crucial to talk to your mentor about these various pieces of advice in order to better understand why he or she provided you with that guidance in the first place.
- It might be difficult to know where to begin if you're feeling overwhelmed by the quantity of chores or exercises your mentor wants you to accomplish on top of your current job.

Discuss this with your mentor. If you're still having trouble prioritising, ask your mentor directly what he or she would recommend you do first!

- Are you looking for an ally, a cheerleader, or a mentor? Sometimes all you need is someone to tell you how great you are, but other times you need someone to be honest with you.
- As mentors, we understand the weight of responsibility that comes with making this connection work. While it is a partnership, and the quality of the working relationship is a shared responsibility, the mentee is responsible for their own learning, progress, and achievement of their goals.
- If a mentor is perceived as uncommitted, skipping meetings and failing to respond to e-mails, the mentee must take action. Remembering that those who have volunteered to be mentors have already made a substantial commitment to the process, the mentee should approach the matter with the mentor. If the mentor is having a very busy period, the mentee might inquire if the mentor wants to check in or arrange phone calls for a few weeks.
- It's critical to raise this with your mentor if you believe he or she isn't devoted to your mentoring relationship. Someone who has committed to being a mentor usually has a strong dedication to the process, so their seeming lack of attention or devotion may surprise you.
- As a mentor, you must also provide direction, balance, and challenge. And if you are only focused on your mentee's objective, such traits may be harmed.
- Setting up the dialogue with strong best practise is a great technique here. Remind the mentee of the importance of secrecy and timeliness, in addition to establishing safety and rapport.
- Because you don't want to disappoint anyone, the situation is typically exacerbated. One solution is to take the list of assignments to your mentors individually and ask them to assist you in prioritising your duties. Better yet, schedule a team

meeting so your mentors may discuss the importance of duties with one another.

- It may be beneficial for you to speak with peers in order to get a better understanding of the level of direction they are receiving.
- When the mentee has a thorough knowledge of the topic and is willing to address it with the mentor, the mentee is ready to proceed.

"Mentoring is a brain to pick, a ear to listen and just that slight push in the right direction." - John Crosby

Actionable For Mentor

- Avoid scheduling mishaps as much as possible. One of the most common challenges that mentors and mentees face is scheduling. In today's hyper-connected, over-scheduled culture, it's tough to imagine squeezing in another meeting.
- Engagement and trust are inextricably linked. As a result, focus on fundamental factors such as confidentiality in sessions and integrity outside of sessions. Stick to your agreements. Also, be willing to provide some personal details about yourself.
- If a mentee is perceived to be weak in dedication, it is critical for the mentor to strive to determine the root problem. It's possible that the mentee-mentor match isn't working out, or that the mentee has realised that his or her professional goal is no longer interesting.
- When presented with a difficult challenge, a competent mentor painstakingly teaches his or her mentee to think and act independently and to discover the resources needed.
- Remember, spoon-feeding would teach your mentee little more than the form of the spoon in the long run. Mentorship is, after all, the art of fostering understanding.
- Simply matching two people for a mentorship program might lead to disappointment for everyone involved. When you identify clear goals, devise means to track progress, and set critical milestones, the experience will be more rewarding.

- Mentors must be extra cautious to ensure that their mentee does not develop an unhealthy reliance on them as the connection develops.
- To avoid falling into this trap, begin by honing the skill of recognising that feeling of anxiety about giving value in the present moment. Then, to break those cognitive habits, note how much more emphasis is placed on the self than on the mentee.
- Remember, mentorship, on the other hand, is not a cloning machine. If you try to xerox yourself, you'll simply miss out on new insights and opportunities that others can provide.
- Too much support can overwhelm a mentee and foster dependency, while too little support might *"leave the mentee floundering"* and stymie progress toward independence.
- When the mentee understands the problem and is ready to address it with the mentor, the mentee should do so. The mentor will be sensitive to your issues if you have a trusting connection and employ strong communication skills.
- Move beyond any roadblock in your next mentoring conversation by getting you and your mentee clear on the higher-level goal that brought you together, and then temporarily adopting that agenda as your own.
- Chat about your personal life with your mentee, eat a meal with them to develop a human connection. Too much formality or a single-minded focus on work might stifle the growth of honesty and trust.
- Putting it out there is a fantastic way to handle the possible issue of dependence. Bring it up with your mentee at the start of the mentoring endeavour, and then on a frequent basis throughout the relationship.
- Stay ahead of the game in the future. From the beginning, set clear expectations. Finally, don't just get together for the sake of getting together.
- Mentee force you to think about things differently, challenge your beliefs, and ask probing questions, which is why mentoring

is so important to him. So, let's think about mentorship in a new light. It's not only about helping others; it's about investing in your own personal growth as well.

- A potential mentor must carefully assess his or her available time and desire to devote to the mentoring process.

Summing Up

Mentorship is the skill of unlocking potential in others. In order to maintain your position of relative authority, you may unintentionally slip into the crippling errors of mentorship. The most effective mentoring relationships are those that develop naturally. Outstanding mentors will be awestruck by how their mentees go about accomplishing what they do. Motivating mentors is one of the most difficult issues that workplace mentoring programs face. Many people place a high value on mentoring, but genuinely outstanding mentors understand that their mentees will teach them as much as they will educate them. Mentors must be willing to devote a considerable amount of time and effort to the program, as well as possess the necessary abilities and insights to impart to their mentee. As a mentor, you must provide direction, balance, and challenge to your mentee. Setting up the dialogue with strong best practise is a great technique here. If the mentor is having a very busy period, the mentee might inquire if the mentor wants to arrange phone calls for a few weeks. Mentorship is, after all, the art of fostering understanding.

CHAPTER FOUR

LEADING YOUR ORGANIZATION TO SUCCESS

"Mentors have a way of seeing more of our faults that we would like. It's the only way we grow."

- George Lucas

Mentorship in the workplace has many benefits. According to statistics, mentoring is one of the most useful and successful growth opportunities a business can provide its workers. Having a trustworthy and experienced mentor give direction, encouragement, and support may provide a mentee with a wide range of personal and professional advantages, which can lead to greater job performance. Mentorship benefits everyone participating in the program, including the host organization. Mentoring decreases turnover considerably. Turnover costs US firms almost $1 trillion every year on average. Employee replacement costs are astronomically expensive. According to Gallup, the cost of replacing an employee might be as much as two times the employee's income or more. In the oil and gas industry, replacing highly specialised personnel can cost up to 400% of their salary.

Direct Benefits Of Mentorship In An Organization

Benefits To Mentees

- It enables the development of a skill or expertise
- instils confidence in the mentee's capacity to complete the work at hand
- It helps the mentee improve his or her communication skills
- It provides practise taking comments from a consistent source for the mentee
- It shows the mentee how to keep a professional connection going
- The mentee's network of connections is expanded
- It gives you a quick overview of the current corporate culture

Benefits To Mentors

- It helps the mentor improve his or her active listening abilities
- It allows the mentor to contribute back to the organization through a channel
- The mentor is encouraged to share his or her knowledge, which boosts the mentor's self-esteem
- It is recognised that teaching provides a sense of fulfilment
- Assists the mentor in honing his or her relationship-building abilities
- Increases one's sense of purpose and duty in their work

Benefits To Employees

Mentors and mentoring may have a significant influence on an employee's professional growth, career development, and mobility. Employees that are mentored get guidance, counsel, and assistance in order to attain their maximum potential. One way mentors may open doors is by introducing their mentee to crucial individuals in their network. Employees improve their networking skills by participating in group or peer mentoring. Mentors can also educate their mentees how to improve networking skills so that they can succeed in the job. A mentee might not know what actions to take or how to effectively complete certain duties; mentors can help with that. For example, a mentee may approach a mentor who has been assigned a task in the organization about which he or she is unfamiliar, and the mentor will share their knowledge with the mentee. Employees who have a mentor are 5 to 6 times more likely to get promoted than their colleagues. A mentor assists mentees in setting career objectives and developing a plan to achieve them. They give useful input and encouragement along the process.

Benefits To The Organization

- Assists them in meeting their talent development objectives, such as succession planning and good leadership development
- Communicates to all employees that the company's leadership is prepared to invest in them
- Improves the efficacy of talent recruitment initiatives. New employees are aware of the company's professional advancement options
- It encourages staff retention, which can result in lower turnover rates
- As a result of one-on-one engagement, training expenditures are lower
- Increased employee engagement & lower turnover rate
- Increased workplace diversity & increase productivity and earnings
- According to the Bureau of Labor Statistics report for 2021, the current turnover rate is 57.3 percent. With nearly 3 million Americans quitting their jobs every month, it's clear that businesses are having trouble keeping their staff.

According to a 2019 CNBC/SurveyMonkey Workplace Happiness Survey, more than four out of every ten workers without a mentor considered quitting their job in the previous three months.Mentorship, on the other hand, has been shown to be an effective way to reduce turnover. Mentees (72%) and mentors (69%) had significantly higher retention rates than workers who did not participate in the mentoring program (49%). Implementing a mentoring program will raise an organization's productivity since mentorship, when done correctly, helps a mentee focus on their strengths and shortcomings while also boosting their confidence and performance. Mentoring increased productivity in 67 percent of organizations. Employee development opportunities are the second most significant factor in determining engagement. Furthermore, according to Brad Johnson, co-author of the book "The Elements of Mentoring," over fifty years of study reveals that people who have exceptional mentors do better and have higher performance ratings than those who try to do it on their own. Mentorship is a two-way street. Employees require friendships at work in order to thrive. People who have close ties with their peers are 50% happier. They're also seven times more likely to be enthusiastic about their jobs. A Gallup poll showed that mentoring programs are one of numerous strategies to retain and engage 94 percent of millennials at work. Because millennials prioritise employment that has a clear value and offers an opportunity for personal or professional advancement, this is the case. Mentors provide millennial employees with the assistance and guidance they require to advance. Mentorship in the workplace is a common approach for organizations to effectively incorporate new employees into the firm. However, these initiatives can and should be much more than a tool for onboarding. Strong mentorship programs not only benefit new recruits but also serve to foster an open, welcoming culture that encourages all employees to share their ideas for enhancing the organization. In a new Accountemps analysis, 93 percent of workers polled said goal setting is vital to their job performance, yet for some professionals, such meetings with supervisors never happen.Some companies make the mistake of allowing new employees to shadow older employees in the hopes that important information will be communicated organically.

Mentoring connections are beneficial to more than just mentees. Team members who actively participate in coaching and advising others have the chance to hone their leadership abilities and demonstrate their preparedness to take on further responsibilities in front of senior management. One of the most important rewards of mentoring relationships, according to mentors, is the gratification of helping others—paying it forward. Mentoring programs are one of the most effective (and least expensive) methods for a firm to foster employee loyalty and engagement. High turnover rates can be decreased, productivity can be boosted, and your team's skill set can be broadened. Turnover may be expensive. By investing in a workplace mentorship program, you may demonstrate to employees that you care about their professional growth. This is an excellent approach to increasing employee loyalty while decreasing high turnover rates. Employee productivity is increased via mentorship. Mentorships assist people in feeling happy at work. This motivates them to work harder and take pride in their work. Mentorships and other career development programs can help your team members improve the talents they bring to the table. Workplace mentoring programs assist both the mentor and the mentee to develop soft skills. These programs can also assist high-performing individuals in reaching their full potential within your firm. Investing in a workplace mentorship program allows your firm to reap the benefits of the beneficial influence. However, if you let the hustle of reopening your office push your mentoring program to the backburner until a later date, you will miss out on these advantages. You will also have to start from scratch and rebuild your workplace mentorship program if you decide to discontinue it.

Limitations

Some companies make the mistake of allowing new employees to shadow older employees in the hopes that important information will be communicated organically.You'll need data to make a solid match. Creating a questionnaire that questions interested workers about their career goals, communication styles, and what they want in a mentor or mentee is one method to gather information. Mentor-mentee relationships that work are ones in which the members share common interests and personalities, as well as complementing aims. Make mentoring a priority in your company's culture. Promote it during the hiring process, begin pairing new hires with mentors during orientation, and ensure that the pairings are given the resources they need to succeed. This necessitates extensive preparation, internal marketing, training, and follow-up. Ensure that top-level executives promote the program, underline its relevance, and are active participants. Maintain straightforward, uncomplicated, and upbeat communication. Make it clear that involvement is entirely optional, but emphasise the value of mentoring for both professional development and the company's bottom line. After launch, don't expect the application to operate on autopilot. Inquire about each participant's input on a frequent basis, and look for ways to enhance processes. Make a point of gathering success stories and testimonials in order to promote the program in the future. Mentoring programs and relationships differ not just from one company to the next, but also from one person to the next. It's critical, though, that everyone understands that "mentor" is not the same as "supervisor." Mentors provide advice and assistance rather than assigning tasks or telling mentees how to execute their professions.

Mentorship Program- Planning & Design

In a business, company, or academic context, a formal mentoring program is an organised, generally one-to-one connection. A well-functioning mentoring program needs strategic preparation and management to connect individuals, improve knowledge, and build skills for future objectives and milestones. Mentoring programs that are effective teach mentors and mentees how to have good talks and meetings while also providing them with career development tools and resources to help them achieve their objectives. Identifying the program's purpose and vision, understanding your mentor and mentee pool candidates while incorporating periodic participant check-ins, and consistent communication and promotion to encourage the program's longevity are all necessary for a successful mentoring program to be implemented. When done correctly, a mentorship program in a professional context can be a fun and fulfilling experience for both corporations and their employees.

Any mentorship program should begin with the following two key questions:

1. What prompted you to start this program?
2. What does it mean to be successful for both the participants and the organization?

Convert your vision into SMART goals that are specific, measurable, achievable, relevant, and time-bound. Objectives provide program participants with direction, define program key performance indicators (KPIs), and explain why organizational leaders should support the program. Mentorship programs that work include structure as well as freedom. Structure provides participants with a mentoring procedure to follow, which is essential for achieving productive learning that meets established objectives. Flexibility is also necessary to meet varied individual mentoring requirements based on learning objectives, preferences, and learning styles.

Do you want to know how to start a mentorship program? That's fantastic. Mentorship is a tried-and-true method for both mentees and mentors to achieve rich learning and growth. Mentorship has a positive impact on the sponsoring organization as well. Mentorship improves employee retention, advancement rates, and happiness for companies. When institutions use alumni as mentors, student mentoring has been shown to promote student retention, increase job placement rates, and increase alumni involvement. Mentoring programs of this kind don't just appear out of nowhere. They're made possible by careful preparation and a long-term commitment to assisting participants through the mentoring process while also refining the program. Choosing to develop a mentorship program is a terrific way to improve staff retention and other metrics. According to a PeopleFluent survey, 78 percent of millennials reported that participating in a mentoring program helped them feel more involved with their company. Furthermore, BambooHR discovered that providing "an employee buddy or mentor" was one of the most critical things a new employee required to come up to speed and start contributing quickly for 56 percent of new recruits.

Even the world's finest entrepreneurs, as evidenced by the examples above, require mentoring in order to shine brighter. Naveen Tewari, the founder and CEO of InMobi Group, India's first unicorn, was coached by Dr. Tarun Khanna, a Harvard Business School professor. Professor Khanna has researched how entrepreneurship may help emerging markets flourish socially and economically. His thoughts helped me see the bigger picture of the work we were doing. "*When I was driving InMobi, it showed me the value of dreaming big as an entrepreneur and solving large issues,*" says Tewari. The learning that began a decade ago has continued with Prof Khanna coming on InMobi's board. "*The experience and expertise of a long time mentor like Prof. Khanna is invaluable for the company*", he added.

Tweet: "*Believed that women micro entrepreneurs can fuel job creation in rural areas when given appropriate financial support and mentoring. With his support, Bharatiya Yuva Shakti Trust has created hundreds of women Grampreneurs across all regions." -Rahul Bajaj*

The other day, Bill Gates met Warren Buffet for the first time in July 1991, albeit unwillingly. Buffet is still one of Bill Gates' closest friends and mentors after 30 years. Business, economics, politics, international events, and philanthropy bring the two together. During Mark Zuckerberg's early days as an entrepreneur, Steve Jobs was his go-to person. At Jobs' request, Zuckerberg visited a temple in Uttarakhand and spent a month in India to see how people interacted. As a result of the experience, he had a greater understanding of the significance and relevance of his venture. Sir William Crookes was an excellent experimenter, the inventor of the vacuum tube, and the discoverer of helium. He was also a very spiritual individual who experimented with the paranormal on a regular basis. Someone as astute as him had to be on to something. Nikola Tesla admired him and learned a lot from him. He was inspired by him and pursued his studies. Crookes, for his part, stood by Tesla's side, protecting him when the world turned against him at one point. Sir William Crookes was a chemist and physicist who studied at London's Royal College of Chemistry. After the discovery of the vacuum tube in 1875, he was regarded as a pioneer. He then invented the Crookes radiometer, which is still sold as a novelty item today. The radiometer, also known as a light mill, is made up of an airtight glass bulb with a partial vacuum inside of it. Following up on Crookes' findings, Tesla discovered that Radiant the Mentoring Manager could also transmit electrostatic charges. While business-driven skill changes are one element of the equation, emotional intelligence, cultural adaptation, strategic intent, physical health, financial acumen, and other factors all become part of holistic personal development and are incorporated into organised and unstructured strategies. As a result of this approach to work, a people manager's position will change from that of a supervisor to that of a mentor. A good mentor can serve as a link between personal and corporate goals, as well as extrinsic and intrinsic motivation. One of the most amazing aspects of a successful mentoring program is the extent to which beneficial ripple effects may be felt. When employees' own needs and the needs of the organization are in sync, they are happy, engaged, and productive. Salary and benefits may be sufficient to entice top talent into the door, but they will not be sufficient to retain or motivate them to do their best work.Employees attain their full potential when their employment provides intrinsic incentives, such as the satisfaction of doing important work that contributes to their personal and professional growth.One of the most amazing aspects of a successful mentoring program is the extent to which beneficial ripple effects may be felt. Mentorship improves an organization by increasing employee happiness and retention while also assisting the mentee's personal and professional development.

Furthermore, a Harvard Business Review survey of 30 professional organizations found that mentorship programs can easily become monotonous and bureaucratic in a hypercompetitive industry.

• Employees who participated in the program were five times more likely to advance in their pay grade, and mentors advanced even faster.

• Mentors were promoted five times more than non-mentees, while mentees were promoted six times more.

• Mentees (72%) and mentors (69%) had significantly higher retention rates than non-participating personnel (49%).

Mentoring programs increased minority presence in management by 9 percent to 24 percent, according to Cornell University's School of Industrial and Labor Relations (compared to 2 percent to 18 percent with other diversity initiatives), according to the same study.boosted minorities' and women's promotion and retention rates by 15 percent to 38 percent when compared to non-mentored employees.

Building Mentoring Culturc

A mentoring culture allows firms to bring on board not only profitable but also fascinating ideas, boosting their innovation quotient and giving them a competitive advantage. However, how will they make the transition from management to mentorship? Management's approach has long since vanished. The old approach to leading a team no longer works, especially as the younger generation enters the job. Leaders must recognise the peculiarities of the younger generation, as well as the reality that they are naturally gifted in certain areas, such as technology. This acknowledgement is the first step toward mentorship from management.

Prahlad Kakar, AD Film Director, Founder Genesis Film Production said at the recently held People Matters Total Rewards and Wellness Conclave 2019, "Mentorship is not about telling people what to do. It is about partnering." Prahlad Kakar adds, "Mentorship is a two-way process, you both learn and teach. In fact, mentors often learn more than they teach." The Founder of Genesis Film Production spoke on the topic "Management to Mentorship" at the People Matters Total Rewards and Wellness Conclave 2019.

The key to mentorship is to take one stride forward and one step back, and to have the bravery and humility to learn from someone who may be less experienced, but who is more competent and well-equipped in their field. Mentorship is about defending that brilliant idea that everyone else is stifling. At the end of the day, directly rejecting an employee's suggestion in front of the executives has a negative influence on employee engagement, productivity, and, at the end of the day, the business. On the other hand, the benefits of recognising and supporting an idea and providing it with the resources it needs to thrive are breathtaking.

According to a recent study by HR.Com, The State of Coaching and Mentoring 2020, as firms try to replace the informal interactions that existed before the epidemic, mentoring will rise dramatically over the next two years, according to a recent study by HR.Com. According to the report, the present mentorship is useless. The problem that firms face is establishing and maintaining a mentorship program that will improve performance and engagement, as well as profit and creativity. Mentoring also boosts "organizational citizenship behaviour," which means individuals treat each other well and help one another, according to Ellen Esher, author of "Power Mentoring: How Successful Mentors and Protégés Get the Most Out of Their Relationships." One of the most effective ways to establish and promote a more inclusive workplace is through a mentorship program. Mentoring relationships are social exchanges that must be mutually beneficial and reciprocal.

Business analyst Leticia shares, "Until I joined McKinsey, I did not know the difference between mentors and sponsors. I learned quickly that mentors are the people you'll reach out to for advice, whenever you feel bad or have to make a difficult decision, they will provide you guidance, or at least emotional comfort. Sponsors, on the other hand, are the ones who will proactively create opportunities for you to advance in your career, they'll push you to expand your limits and provide coaching to develop professional skills."

Mentoring in a VUCA environment

Welcome to the VUCA world if you're wondering why tactics or strategies that seemed to work in the past don't seem to work today, or why certain activities don't have the expected outcomes. VUCA is an acronym that stands for Very Urgent Critical Action. Uncertainty, chaos, and ambiguity characterise this situation. And there are no predictable responses in a VUCA environment. So, in a VUCA environment, how do you mentor? Mentoring in a VUCA world is less about giving solutions and more about assisting them in finding answers. In this VUCA environment where there are no predictable solutions, mentoring is about assisting your mentee in becoming more comfortable with not having all the answers and giving them the courage to find the answers on their own. We're all struggling with temporal compression, and the higher we climb the corporate ladder, the more filtered the data becomes. When you mentor strategically throughout the business, you get a sense of what's important, you acquire real-time data, and that, at the end of the day, is what will offer your company a competitive edge.

Best Practices- Mentorship In An Organization

1. Establish ground rules and expectations.One of the difficulties with mentorship programs is that mentees sometimes do not know what to anticipate from the experience. They may turn to mentors to set their goals for them, or they may realise that the people involved do not agree on how frequently to meet.

Creating a voluntary, employee-driven mentorship system can assist in avoiding these dangers. We're upfront about the time commitment required at Dataminr, and we ask that participants meet at least once a month for six months.

Participants go through a systematic application process and training program, and we provide tactical templates and a monthly budget for off-site sessions, resulting in a more tailored and effective experience.

2. Seek assistance from a leader.Another challenge that many businesses confront is a lack of stakeholder support for their mentorship programs. Busy mentors may not prioritise their dedication to their mentees, which can have a detrimental influence on the program's success rates as well as staff morale. As a result, it is critical to secure the support of top leadership who are on board with the program as soon as feasible.

Whether these leaders provide a budget, advocate for workers to participate, or encourage other senior leaders to sign up, leadership support is the lifeblood of these sorts of initiatives and demonstrates to employees how much senior management values their success.

As a result, it is critical to secure the support of top leadership who are on board with the program as soon as feasible. Whether these leaders provide a budget, advocate for workers to participate, or encourage other senior leaders to sign up, leadership support is the lifeblood of these sorts of initiatives and demonstrates to employees how much senior management values their success.

3. Collect feedback as soon as possible and as frequently as possible.Aside from their monthly meetings, program participants should be encouraged to share their thoughts on their experiences. Companies that do not set key performance indicators (KPIs) and gather feedback are passing up an opportunity to optimise for better results. Dataminr, for its part, collects both qualitative and quantitative feedback every eight weeks through three feedback sessions in each 6-month program. We advocate conducting brief questionnaires to measure participant satisfaction, determine how much they appreciate the program, and determine how much it affects their job.

4. Assign your program's responsibility to a single team.A mentoring program must be part of a certain team inside your business in order to function well. It is up to these team members to advocate for the program, assess its progress, and accept responsibility for its outcomes. This job frequently overlaps with the activities of human resources (HR). HR (or a comparable people-focused team) can pilot its success by supporting the application process, finding meaningful connections, supervising the program's orientation training, and ensuring that participants prioritise their engagement.

5. Assign your program's responsibility to a single team.A mentoring program must be part of a certain team inside your business in order to function well. It is up to these team members to advocate for the program, assess its progress, and accept responsibility for its outcomes. This job frequently overlaps with

the activities of human resources (HR). HR (or a comparable people-focused team) can pilot its success by supporting the application process, finding meaningful connections, supervising the program's orientation training, and ensuring that participants prioritise their engagement.

If your mentoring program hasn't succeeded in the past, it's likely because it lacked the structure and accountability required to foster the proper degree of participation. By implementing these best practises, you can transform this opportunity for learning and growth into a strategy for increasing employee happiness, engagement, and retention—and, as a result, position your business for future growth.

HR Role In Organizational Mentorship

Mentorship is one of the most underappreciated and underutilized talent management techniques. Mentorship has the potential to help individuals for a lifetime. According to a recent study by HR.Com, The State of Coaching and Mentoring 2020, as firms try to replace the informal interactions that existed before the epidemic, mentoring will rise dramatically over the next two years, according to a recent study by HR.Com. According to the report, the present mentorship is useless. The problem that firms face is establishing and maintaining a mentorship program that will improve performance and engagement, as well as profit and creativity. Mentoring also boosts "organizational citizenship behaviour," which means individuals treat each other well and help one another, according to Ellen Esher, author of "Power Mentoring: How Successful Mentors and Protégés Get the Most Out of Their Relationships." One of the most effective ways to establish and promote a more inclusive workplace is through a mentorship program. Mentoring relationships are social exchanges that must be mutually beneficial and reciprocal.

Summing Up

Mentors and mentoring may have a significant influence on an employee's professional growth. Employees who have a mentor are 5 to 6 times more likely to get promoted than their colleagues.

When done correctly, mentorship helps a mentee focus on their strengths and shortcomings while boosting their confidence and performance. People who have close ties with their peers are 50% happier. Promote mentoring during the hiring process and ensure that the pairings are given the resources they need to succeed. Mentorship is one of the most underappreciated and underutilized talent management techniques. Mentors provide advice and assistance rather than assigning tasks or telling mentees how to execute their professions. Establishing and maintaining a mentorship program will improve employees' performance and engagement.

CHAPTER FIVE

EXPECTATIONS BUILDING IN MENTORSHIP

"Mentors, by far, are the most important aspect of businesses."
-Daymond John

Avoiding Surprises In Mentorship

When you enter a new scenario, it helps to know what to expect. You may look up material on the Internet, talk to friends and family, or do other things to learn more so that you aren't startled or anxious throughout the event. Mentorship is no exception. Setting expectations from the outset will allow both parties to be calm, honest, and at ease in order to get the most out of the encounter. What comes to your mind when you think of, when people think of, when you use the words *"mentoring"* and *"expectations"*? What do you believe are some of the most common misunderstandings about that? because you're going to do something for them and the company. Individuals generally start mentoring partnerships with presumptuous expectations of one another, which are seldom acknowledged. It's virtually impossible to accomplish goals that you don't even know exist if expectations aren't laid out. A lack of expectations will only result in dissatisfaction, missed opportunities, and challenging discussions based on assumptions. Expectations must be distinct, simple, and unambiguous. You'll also look at some other requirements to guarantee that the mentoring connection is fruitful. When expectations are not stated or defined, many people feel frustrated and or disappointed with their mentoring relationships. To avoid dissatisfaction in your mentoring relationship, set some realistic expectations straight away. Mentors and mentees frequently learn that their expectations are similar or identical, and they can always go back to them if required. Finally, it is critical to recognise that mentoring relationships are partnerships, and reciprocal support and respect are required for healthy partnerships.

While every mentoring relationship is unique, there are certain common tasks and obligations shared by both the mentor and the mentee. However, while they are widespread, they are not universal; you should be clear with your mentoring partner about your expectations and obligations. Nothing is more stressful for a mentor than attempting to assist a mentee who is not doing what they pledged to do. Some mentors approach mentoring as though they can mould and sculpt their mentee into their ideal, much like Michelangelo did with David. Let me be clear about something. This is the incorrect method. You can not force your mentee to become someone they are not. And they cannot and should not attempt to imitate your line of work.If you want to be an inspirational mentor, you can't approach mentoring as if your mentees are all the same. For example, we frequently ask mentees to read a book and return in a month to discuss it. Similarly, we may offer a candidate a few weeks to write a review of a paper in a related field. In a corporate situation, you may ask a prospective mentee to prepare a presentation in their area of expertise, or you may invite them to accompany you on a sales call or during a strategy offsite and write down their views.

With so many of the world's most notable executives going on record to thank a mentor for part of their success, the relationship between a mentor and a mentee can be the most influential in business. As you know, Sir Freddie Laker, Richard Branson's mentor, was instrumental in getting Virgin Atlantic off the ground. If you ask any thoroughbred professional to name the top three most important factors in their success, there's a good chance they'll include a mentor, who is an experienced person who served as a trusted advisor while the professional progressed up the corporate ladder. It is up to both the mentor and the mentee to make the most of the relationship, whether it is part of a structured employee mentoring programme or an informal mentoring relationship. Be wary of the hesitant applicant who wants the mentor to maintain the connection or the candidate who insists on doing things their way. A mentee should be inquisitive, organized, efficient, accountable, and engaged. Expectations and surprises in building a mentorship programs creating a structured, in-house mentoring programs is an important talent development strategy. Here are some of the most common actionables to avoid surprises in mentorship.

- An excellent workplace mentorship programme will include conversation prompts in the form of a series of questions or tasks to steer the discussion.
- The initial session should start with a discussion on what the mentee hopes to gain from the relationship, their career development objectives, and how they believe they can realise their full potential rather than the other way around.
- Egos have no place in this sort of connection, on either the mentor or the mentee side.
- Mentees should feel supported and in command of their own personal and professional objectives.
- Mentors should be honest about what they can do for their mentees and let them understand what sort of aid they may anticipate.
- A successful mentoring programme should take care to match mentors with mentees for a good fit.
- Please ensure your mentee must follow through on action items that may arise as a consequence of mentorship discussions, as well as be prepared for meetings with their mentor.

- A mentor's responsibility is to listen, determine what a mentee requires, and encourage them in their development. Curiosity is an essential character quality for every effective mentor.
- An excellent workplace mentorship programme will include conversation prompts in the form of a series of questions or tasks to steer the discussion.
- It is critical to recognise that each connection is unique – even within an employee development programme.
- It is crucial to emphasise that mentors are not there to assign work and handle issues in the same capacity as someone's supervisor.
- A mentor serves as trustworthy counsel. Anything spoken during a session should be kept strictly confidential.
- As a mentor or mentee, it's best not to pretend to know everything. That may destroy the sense of curiosity and openness to explore through collaborative problem solving.
- A mentor's strength resides in their expertise and desire to collaborate with a mentee to achieve common goals.
- Mentors should provide insight and direction. If you are unwilling to do so in a way that benefits your mentee, both of you will benefit from the experience.
- Setting objectives for both the long-term and short-term; for what the mentee wants to accomplish personally and professionally, skill sets they want to work on, and a direction for the relationship to flourish as part of the initial session.
- As a mentor you should concentrate on opportunities for progress and overcome professional obstacles rather than personal defects.
- Take the initiative in the connection, organising all meetings and driving the mentee's progress. Continue the relationship after the agreed-upon time span has passed.
- The best method to accomplish mentorship goals is to question existing thinking and assist mentees in growing.
- Talking too much regardless of expertise, each mentoring session should be a back-and-forth discussion in which the

mentor stimulates critical thinking and self-evaluation.

- The frequency with which these messages are carried out is just as significant as the mode of communication. The frequency with which they meet will be determined by the intricacy of the difficulties, the amount of time each has to provide, and the mentee's overall development.
- Mentors must be able to evaluate whether they have enough time on their calendar to prioritise their mentee for the period allotted.
- As with any excellent business plan, mentors and mentees should collaborate to determine what success looks like and what indicators should be monitored.
- Simply telling people what to do destroys a large element of the mentor-mentee connection in which you work together to overcome problems and progress.
- It is not your responsibility as a mentor to devise a strategy for your mentee. Instead, you must insist that your mentees have their own objectives and strategies. You, as a motivating mentor, will not make the strategy. You will assist your mentee in refining their strategy.
- Be flexible because participants may have preconceived notions about what a mentor-mentee relationship should include. It is critical to recognise that each connection is unique – even within an employee development programme.
- Please remember that each mentor brings distinct abilities and experiences to the table, and each mentee faces unique obstacles while pursuing varied career and personal goals.
- Effective mentoring is discipline-agnostic. Mentorship takes time to be effective. Mentors spend hours that they could be using to accomplish their own professional objectives on someone else's. So, pick your mentee wisely.
- Your personal development stories can motivate mentees and urge them to open up.
- The mentor-mentee connection should be founded on honesty and constructive feedback, as well as providing a secure

environment for mentees to use their mentor as a sounding board.

- Please remember, your professional and mentoring experience and guidance will be invaluable in improving leadership skills. So, whether you're interviewing for a new post, becoming more involved with the business culture, or gathering the courage to talk with your senior management.
- Maintains a professional relationship with the mentee that does not interfere with the mentee's personal life and does not expect to be good friends with the mentee.
- Finally, emphasise that accountability is not optional. Effective mentors teach mentees about professional standards and guarantee that they meet them. Deadlines must be met, project commitments must be followed, and appointment times must be kept.

Now that you know what mentors and mentees commonly expect of one another, you will be given a template to create your own list of mentoring expectations. You can use any of the expectations you've read about or create your own set of expectations. For that, you have to send personal request to the author. In addition to these general mentoring expectations, you and your mentoring partner may have certain mentorship-specific expectations. For example, a mentoring pair may agree to attend conferences or other events together, or to allow the mentee to work shadow. These extra mentoring requirements can aid in the growth of the mentee. The trick is to make these mentoring standards explicit; discuss them, agree on them, and even put them in writing. Mentoring expectations are thus not left unspoken—and hence unsatisfied. In my experience, the most effective partnerships are those in which the mentee completely understands and shares their mentor's goal for success.

Mentor's Responsibilities In Mentorship

- You must take the initiative in the relationship but allow the mentee to take responsibility for their own growth, development, and career planning.
- You need to determine what your mentee expects from the relationship, compare it to your expectations, and reach an agreement.
- You may be underestimating the mentee's long-term aspirations, while the mentee may overestimate the services you will provide. Such misconceptions are costly in terms of both time and peace of mind. These disagreements should be addressed honestly and early on in any mentoring relationship.
- Commits to meeting with mentee on a regular basis, preferably outside of the mentee's working hours; no less than one hour per month.
- You must actively listens to the mentee and provides candid, honest, and constructive feedback.
- You must motivates the mentee and assists him or her in identifying professional development opportunities.
- You must maintains anonymity while recognising and resolving conflicts in a caring manner, invites discussion of differences with the mentee, and arranges for a third party to assist if necessary.
- Only make positive or neutral comments about the mentee to others; if there is a disagreement about behaviour or ideals, communicate differences with the mentee; if necessary, end the relationship and find another mentor for the mentee.
- Ask for details and, if necessary, guidance. Recognize that any suggestion isn't definitive and may not be appropriate for you. The more significant a matter is, the more critical it is to carefully analyse it with counsel and seek second and third perspectives.
- Be open to engaging in fruitful debates and different approaches to teaching and professional responsibilities.
- Be honest about any minor issues you're having with your mentoring relationship. If things aren't working out, accept the

truth and employ a "no blame" breakup policy if the mentoring year isn't finished.

- As your mentee progress toward independence, you as mentor should investigate what their mentees require and assist them in striking a constructive balance between asking for assistance and taking on greater responsibility.
- Make use of email, the phone, and face-to-face time. Bring any questions, misunderstandings, concerns, or issues you may have. Bring accomplishments, alternatives, and ideas as well.
- Meet as frequently as necessary. Planning ahead of time, being spontaneous, or a combination of the two are all acceptable options as long as they benefit you both.
- Make it clear what you require, and express your dissatisfaction with any particular behaviour or idea. Stick to topics that are actually interesting to you.

Mentee's Responsibilities In Mentorship

- At the outset, you must specify the exact requirement or topic for which you are seeking help. This assists both the mentor and the mentee in determining the likelihood of a reciprocal connection.
- Determine if you want a one-time commitment for a single piece of advice or an ongoing connection. A busy mentor may be willing to help you with a specific problem but will not have time for a long-term connection.
- Please don't expect your mentor to know everything or to be able to assist you in every scenario. If you require assistance, however, please contact your mentor as soon as possible. It is critical to get assistance from your mentor in overcoming self-doubt.
- You must appreciate the time of your mentors. Setting up an agenda ahead of sessions and ensuring that mentors have enough time to study any associated documents are essential mentee practises. You might look for a new mentor or seek

informal support. Take charge of your relationship. Invite your mentor to a meeting, provide topics for discussion, and specify what you want.

- Understand your own personality and temperament, and recognise that what makes your coworkers happy may not make you happy.
- When you meet with your mentor, keep in mind that her/his time, like yours, is limited, so make the most of your time together.
- Preparation ahead of time; questions that will elicit the knowledge and learning you seek from a mentoring exchange.
- Understand that plans can be altered and that roadmaps might occasionally deviate.
- Be adaptive and don't be scared to change or take on new challenges. Be adaptable and creative.
- Don't give up in the face of criticism. Take criticism as a light prod to keep you on course.
- Develop your ability to manage your time efficiently and to adhere to agreed-upon meeting schedules, deadlines, roles, and duties.
- Take and absorb your mentor's advice. Sort through the lessons and look for trends.
- Significant loss occurs in a matter of hours. Review things in your thoughts as soon as they occur. Prepare for the meeting and consult with individuals who have a relationship with the mentor to overcome your fear.
- Take charge of your own professional development. Your mentor can only point you in the right direction. The ultimate decisions must be made by you, and the final acts are your responsibility.
- Summarize what you learned from your mentor, pay close attention to criticism, and ask clarifying questions.

Summing Up

Setting expectations from the outset will allow both mentor and mentee to be calm, honest, and at ease in order to get the most out of the encounter. Expectations must be distinct, simple, and unambiguous, and reciprocal support and respect are required. If you want to be an inspirational mentor, you can't approach mentoring as if your mentees are all the same. Expectations and surprises in building mentorship programmes are an important talent development strategy. Mentors and mentees should work together to devise a strategy for success. Maintaining a professional relationship with the mentee does not interfere with the mentor's personal life. You can use this template to create your own list of expectations. Make the most of your time as a mentee when you meet with your mentor. Don't expect your mentor to know everything or to assist you in every scenario. It's better to set up an agenda ahead of sessions and ensure that mentors have enough time to study any associated documents that are essential for mentee practice.

CHAPTER SIX

MENTORING RELATIONSHIP

"One of the greatest values of mentors is the ability to see ahead what others cannot see and to help them navigate a course to their destination." -
John C. Maxwell

Building Relationship

When looking at mentor-mentee relationships, it's important to remember that the mentor-mentee connection is a two-way street. When Larry Page and Sergey Brin launched Google, they had no clue how swiftly the firm would grow in the face of their search engine's meteoric rise to become the world's most popular online finder of things. The two were computer scientists, not businesspeople, and they clearly needed an overseer to manage the multi-million pound company's corporate needs. Eric Schmidt, formerly of Sun Microsystems and Novell, was brought in to impress Page and Brin with his open-mindedness. When considering mentor-mentee relationships and critical interactions that helped create the groundwork for some of the contemporary world's most pivotal moments, Steve Jobs's urging Mark Zuckerberg to visit India may not seem all that significant. But it was this tidbit of conversation—specifically, Jobs' suggestion that Zuckerberg visit the same Kainchi Dham temple that he visited during Apple's early gestation period—that propelled Facebook to prominence as the world's most popular communication platform.

"Early on in our history," Zuckerberg added, "when things weren't really going well." "We were going through a rough stretch, and a lot of individuals were interested in buying Facebook."

Great mentors are frequently descended from a lineage of mentors. Consider how wonderful it is to be developing your own great bloodline as you grow your relationship with your mentee. You're educating yourself and mentally preparing for your meeting with your mentee. The Law of Similarity states that individuals like and give more favourable attributes to those who appear to be highly similar to them. People initially see surface-level similarities. People care about things like ethnicity, gender, and where you went to school first. This can be problematic since superficial resemblance might affect our impressions of one another. However, there is some really interesting scientific news. People's opinions of deep-level resemblance become far more relevant than surface-level similarity as they grow to know each other. Deep-level resemblance refers to similarities that cannot be recognised at first glance, such as personality, beliefs, ambitions, world views, and ethics. Good mentor-mentee relationships require effective communication. Agree on regular touchpoints and accountability check-ins. Mentorship takes time, effort, and hard work from both the mentor and the mentee. Without commitment, there will be no discipline to carry out activities or commitments. This will result in the mentoring failing.

"I have heard it said that for older adults, mentoring is about living a legacy versus leaving a legacy"

-David Shapiro, CEO of 'MENTOR' The National Mentoring Partnership

According to research, liking is closely associated with optimism, so if you want to boost your liking for your mentee, be purposely optimistic so they can catch your positivity. While 76 percent of working professionals feel that having a mentor is beneficial to their development, more than 54 percent do not have one. The data on the benefits of mentorship is clear: people who have mentors perform better, advance in their professions faster, and have a better work-life balance. Mentors gain as well. After all, "to teach is to learn twice." Despite all of these benefits, and despite the fact that 76% of working professionals believe having a mentor is critical to their professional development,

People who have comparable interests are more likely to have a fruitful mentoring relationship. This might reflect their ideas and values, educational background, job path, or even where they come from. A good mentoring program will link mentors and mentees with share interests. A competent mentor should be available to his or her mentee at all times. When a mentor's availability for a mentee is highly restricted, it sends a message to the mentee that they aren't a top priority. A mentoring pair could, for example, agree to attend conferences or other events together or enable the mentee to observe the mentor. These extra mentoring requirements can aid in the growth of the mentee. The trick is to make these mentoring expectations clear: talk about them, agree on them, and even write them down in a mentoring contract. Mentoring expectations aren't left unspoken—and unfulfilled—in this way. A mentor-mentee relationship is a two-way professional connection. Both parties have a vested interest in the mentee's success. The mentor does not denigrate or disparage the mentee in any manner; after all, they were once in their mentee's shoes. Similarly, the mentee respects and listens to the mentor's advice and thoughts.

Mentor's Perspective

- Avoid superfluous self-disclosure and attempt to connect your self-disclosure into work, or make a point of doing so with your mentee and urge them to do the same.
- If you can't start a one-on-one connection, consider peer mentoring with coworkers who have similar experiences, issues, and aspirations.
- Group mentoring may be beneficial for groups of workers who want to engage in a more collaborative mentoring process, and it may enable senior institutional leaders who want to mentor to

make the most of their time.

- Maintain a positive attitude and be courteous! Select the appropriate time, location, and situation. Communicate whether you want the self-disclosure to be shared or whether it is only for your mentee's benefit.
- As a mentor, make sure you celebrate every win, no matter how small. On the flip side, never pass up an opportunity to provide constructive feedback, no matter how insignificant it may seem.
- Utilise matching and reciprocity to determine when it is appropriate to self-disclose. So, let's assume a mentee begins to open up to you about something with a low level of danger.
- Sharing something intimate about yourself and matching the amount of risk is one approach to employing reciprocity.
- The mentor must be able to provide constructive comments while also actively listening to determine what the mentee requires.
- While you're self-disclosing, pay attention to your protege's verbal and nonverbal indications. Begin with a lower level of risk and work your way up to the truly delicious stuff.
- If your mentee is preparing for a big presentation, for example, they could welcome some extra help from you.
- Avoid superfluous self-disclosure and attempt to connect your self-disclosure into work, or make a point of doing so with your mentee and urge them to do the same.
- Make sure your motives for becoming a mentor are sound. A mentor should not be in the relationship for the sole purpose of gaining personal benefit.
- Anything the mentee says in the mentoring relationship should be kept private. The mentor and mentee should agree on a set of realistic expectations for the relationship's outcomes. For example, the mentee cannot hold the mentor accountable for achieving the required outcomes.
- Mentorship is more about building relationships than teaching skills. Therefore, the mentor shares their own personal experiences, insights, and expertise with the mentee.

Mentee's Perspective

- The goals of the mentee are the foundation of a mentoring relationship. That implies you're the one who establishes the relationship's goals in the end.
- The mentee is the one who handles the majority of the scheduling and relationship management. Because the mentor cannot predict what mentee will need, you must be honest about what they will need and when they will need it.
- In a mentoring relationship, however, you are not being tested, and you are not required to know all of the answers. A good mentor will ask you some difficult questions, and it's fine if you don't know the answers. Listen to what your mentor has to say and consider how their experiences and hard-learned lessons apply to your present position.
- For a mentee, being able to listen to a practise presentation may make all the difference.
- Look for things you have in common with a mentor to help you build a genuine connection. This might be due to a mutual interest in swing dancing or being from the same city – the options are limitless.
- Mentees require time and space to speak things over and think about them. Moralizing, lecturing, or preaching to your mentee isn't useful. In fact, doing so may compromise the mentoring relationship's success since the mentee may be less willing to discuss their views and difficulties. Because their beliefs and ambitions differ from yours, it's important to meet them where they are rather than impose your own.
- Knowing what role you're intended to perform in the mentoring relationship will set you up for success as a mentee.
- Before meeting with your mentor, look for online mentee training to ensure you're properly prepared.
- A mentee must follow through on action items that may arise as a consequence of mentorship discussions, as well as be prepared for meetings with their mentor.

- Based on your goals for the connection, you'll need to figure out what qualities you'll need from your mentor.
- If a mentor proposes that a mentee read an article, attend a class, or meet with another person, the mentee should do so.
- The mentee should be open to feedback and utilise active listening to ensure that they grasp what is being said to them.
- Nothing irritates a mentor more than attempting to help a mentee who isn't following through on their commitments. If a mentor and mentee discuss a specific issue that the mentee is facing, the mentee should have accomplished the following actions before their next meeting with their mentor.
- It's crucial to establish a good relationship with your mentor. You must be able to open yourself to that individual and be vulnerable in front of them. Talk to them about your worries, your development areas, and the things that are causing you worry.
- Be truthful. Discuss with your mentor what you're having trouble with, what you need help with, and what you'd like your mentor to advise you on. Keep an open mind. This is critical since you will be given criticism, questioned, and may naturally become defensive.
- Develop rapport through self-disclosure For most people, it's a combination of the two. It entails making yourself vulnerable and known to others by sharing your experiences, feelings, and desires.

Flipside In Relationship Building

Unfortunately, there might be a mismatch between a mentor and a mentee. Conflicting personalities, different career objectives or areas of scientific knowledge, variances in work ethic, or any number of other factors may contribute to the mismatch. Fortunately, the mismatch is generally detected early in the relationship by either the mentor or the mentee. The longer the mismatch exists, the more difficult it is to resolve. While finding a mismatch is unfortunate, it is an issue that can be handled, and it is preferable to do so sooner rather than later. If both the mentor and the mentee agree that a change is in order, the mentee can work with his or her division head, department chair, and even the present mentor to make the transition. If both the mentor and the mentee agree that a change is needed, the mentee can collaborate with his or her division chief, department chair, and even the present mentor to find a more suitable mentor.

Your Objective Behind Mentoring Relationship

Knowing what you want from a mentoring relationship Consider the last interview or professional occasion that went really well for you. For a little while, indulge in that fantastic feeling. It's likely that you did well because you prepared well. Preparation is the secret to the most successful encounters. This is especially true when it comes to mentoring. The first stage is to become more self-aware. A 360-degree personal audit is one method for increasing self-awareness. This is my take on the 360-degree performance evaluation. Managers are frequently required by firms to complete 360-degree performance reviews in which they are assessed by their subordinates, colleagues, superiors, and customers. This audit is designed to help you reflect on how others see your strengths and flaws. The second step is to write out your goals. Determine your ambitions, dreams, and long-term objectives over the next six months to five years. Consider the academic, intellectual, health, social, professional, financial, spiritual, or any other aspect of your life that calls to you. Knowing how a mentor can assist you in achieving your objectives can lead you to the correct mentor. Allow whatever ideas or thoughts to enter your head while you take a breath. You might want to go through this again and again. Consider where your ideal mentor works.

- What industry or organization are you referring to?
- Consider reaching out to your mentor. Is it over a cup of coffee, an email, or a networking event?
- How do you feel when you talk to your mentor?
- Consider this a normal chat. How does your mentor assist you?

- What talents will you be able to pick up from your mentor?
- What additional achievements will you have as a result of this relationship?
- What does your ideal mentor resemble?
- Do you have any specific people in mind?

Now go ahead and jot down some notes. Don't worry if you were stuck or didn't know the answers to these questions. Often, the solutions emerge gradually throughout the day, or they become apparent the more times you work through this practise. Clarity is a work in progress. If you continue to take action steps like these, it will become clear who you should contact for a mentor.

Mentoring Relationships- Entry To Exit

The actual action begins now that your participants have been registered, trained, and matched. The mentoring relationship is prone to losing focus and momentum if it lacks direction and strategy. That is why a good mentoring program requires some structure and supervision during the mentoring. Establish checkpoints where mentorship may report on its success as the relationship develops. Even if your company doesn't want to explicitly track the specifics, simply reporting success keeps mentors and mentees on track. Finally, have a clear framework in place to bring the mentoring experience to a close. This provides a chance for both the mentor and the mentee to reflect on what they've learned, talk about future steps for the mentee, and give feedback on the program's advantages.

Starting a mentoring program is a big investment when you consider program administration, infrastructure, and the valuable time of participants. It is critical to articulate the impact in order to secure continuous funding and support. In addition, the measurement phase focuses on measuring the health of the program in order to identify problem areas and possibilities. Mentorship programs that are successful should be recorded, measured, and evaluated at three levels: the program, the mentoring relationship, and the individual. You must be able to collect measurements and input throughout the program's lifespan in order to be effective. You should ask the following questions:

- Is the mentorship period excessively long, excessively short, or just right?
- Are mentorships off to a quick start or stumbling?
- Are participants leveraging the content resources you have provided?

Inquire of participants and stakeholders how well the mentorship program accomplished their and the organization's objectives. Inquire about their suggestions for enhancing the program. Formal mentoring is a powerful method for developing, engaging, and retaining your employees. However, maintaining a successful mentoring program entails much more than simply pairing individuals. True organizational effects need time, money, and expertise. While creating a successful mentoring program from the ground up is no easy undertaking, following the five-step procedure will set you on the right track to achieving your organization's learning objectives. You may make contacts that could lead to opportunities for them as well. Some of these mentorship connections lasted more than a decade, while others were more transient and time-limited. To put it another way, mentoring isn't focused on specific abilities or activities that may be done to enhance them. It's more about long-term progress. Relationships are difficult, and they're made much more difficult when there's a power imbalance, which most mentoring relationships have. So many well-intentioned mentoring partnerships have gone awry because the mentor and the mentee had conflicting expectations. So, with that in mind, let me reveal the four most common mentoring traps so you can detect them early and prevent them. It's critical to find the appropriate individual. Finally, here are some pointers for making the most of your mentoring relationship. I'd like you to schedule meetings on a frequent basis. Every four to eight weeks is good because you get out what you put in. Make preparations for the meeting. Make a list of your goals. These are your meetings. I want you to own it, and I want you to make sure that it covers all you require. By staying in contact artistically, there are so many excellent ways to maintain mentorship ties. Here are some suggestions for preserving the relationship. To begin with, you may always send an email requesting particular types of assistance. Give them a shout-out on social media, for example. Celebrate them publicly when they reach a professional milestone. If they write a paper, a book, or are interviewed, let them know. If you're proud of their professional accomplishments, chances are others will be as well. This behaviour, in turn, reflects positively on you. It all stems from Ann Friedman's Shine Theory notion. When you surround yourself with successful individuals, their light reflects on you as well.

To be honest, mentorship relationships should aim to be symbiotic, mutually helpful, and, to be honest, enjoyable. Be a pleasure to work with, and you'll continue to reap the benefits of a strong network. Here are some suggestions for preserving the relationship. To begin with, you may always send an email requesting particular types of assistance. Request a meeting or phone call to discuss how you're handling a difficult problem at work, get a second set of eyes on your presentation before a big conference, or request a meeting or phone call to discuss how you're handling a sticky situation at work. But you don't want to go to your mentor with a request all of the time. Instead, maintain a reciprocal connection by staying in touch even when you aren't in need.

Momentum in mentoring Helping participants and leadership stay engaged when it comes to your workplace mentorship program may be a problem. Mentoring software, on the other hand, may assist you in developing and managing a successful mentoring program for your firm. Together can help you and your employer stay focused and develop the benefits that come with a strong workplace mentoring program, from registration to matching to tracking and reporting. According to research, if self-disclosure is done effectively, it may enhance professional relationships, engagement, and even be a stress reliever. So, let's get started by following these five stages for employing self-disclosure with your protégé. First, confront your fear. If the thought of disclosing yourself makes you nervous, you are not alone. Many of us are afraid of being judged or of being weak if we are vulnerable, yet being vulnerable with your protégé makes your connection authentic.

Summing Up

Good mentor-mentee relationships require effective communication and accountability check-ins. Mentorship takes time, effort, and hard work from both the mentor and the mentee. A good mentoring program will link mentors and mentees with share interests. A competent mentor should be available to his or her mentee at all times. Both parties have a vested interest in the mentee's success. The trick is to make these mentoring expectations clear. As a mentee, it's important to be prepared for every aspect of the mentoring relationship. Moralizing, lecturing, or preaching to your mentee isn't useful and may compromise their success. Before meeting with your mentor, look for online mentee training to ensure you're properly prepared. It's crucial to establish a good relationship with your mentor. You must be able to open yourself to that individual and be vulnerable in front of them. The mentee should be open to feedback and utilise active listening to ensure they grasp what is being said to them. Mentors and mentees should agree on a set of realistic expectations for the relationship's. The longer the mismatch exists, the more difficult it is to resolve. Knowing how a mentor can assist you in achieving your objectives can lead you to the correct mentor. Starting a mentoring program is a big investment when you consider program administration, infrastructure, and the valuable time of participants. Good mentoring programs that are successful should be recorded, measured, and evaluated at three levels: the program, the mentoring relationship, and the individual. Formal mentoring is a powerful method for developing, engaging, and retaining your employees.

CHAPTER SEVEN

EFFECTIVE GOAL SETTING

"Mentoring is a brain to pick, an ear to listen, and a push into the right direction."

-John C. Crosby

Set SMART Goals With Your Mentees

One of the most valuable gifts we can give others is the capacity to feel fully heard and understood. That's why we become irritated when our loved ones nod along while we're talking, their eyes glued to their smartphones. It's also why we feel better after discussing a difficult subject with someone who listens and empathises. So, when starting a relationship with a new mentee, start by carefully listening and asking plenty of questions to gain a feel for their overall goals. You'll learn more about how to effectively help them this way. Here are four ideas to get you started. Goal-setting Setting goals is an important part of any mentorship, but it can be difficult for both the mentor and the mentee. When a mentee is unsure of what they want to achieve through mentorship, it can be difficult to help them focus. This difficulty can be met in a variety of ways. Begin by encouraging your mentees to apply the SMART goal-setting method. Set a goal that is specific, quantifiable, achievable, reasonable, and time-bound. Mentoring software can assist in tracking objectives so that mentees can see how far they have progressed during the mentoring.

The first stage, whether you're a mentor or a mentee, is to evaluate your own objectives and present professional ties. Consider the following question:

- Who are my current mentors and role models?
- What is it about them that I admire?
- What is it that they all share in common?
- Who has impressed you the most in terms of how they dealt with this or past crises?

Actionables

- Inquire about their short-and long-term job objectives. You get a sense of who they want to be in the coming years and decades.
- Allow room for their ambition by encouraging them to be bold in picturing their life years in the future, without judgement or scepticism.
- Be the voice that encourages them to strive for greater heights. You may work together to establish a low-stakes, secure atmosphere where mentees can explore their aspirations and objectives without fear of being judged.
- Be the sounding board to whom people can turn with both their difficulties and their accomplishments.
- Go over previous performance appraisals. Are they in need of more immediate assistance and hands-on career guidance?
- You may help them think about what they need to learn next by looking at their most recent performance assessment together.
- You might recommend that they attend a class or continue their formal education.
- You may also assist them in role-playing the art of leading a meeting, making a presentation, or cultivating any talent they choose to cultivate.
- It's usually appreciated if you can roll up your sleeves and assist them with troubleshooting in real time.

- Plan how you'll follow up and keep track of progress. Decide how and when you'll stay in touch before your goal-setting meeting ends.
- You may wish to check in on their development on a regular basis to demonstrate your interest and create accountability.

"A great mentor understands the power of having a vision so they can help their mentee develop a personal vision of what they want to achieve." -Lolly Daskal

Introspection- Mentor

- What drives you to be a successful mentor?
- What is it about training that you like the most?
- What makes you want to be a mentor?
- What do you think your greatest strength is?
- How did you learn about your business?
- Is this your job?
- What motivates you to work here?
- What makes you want to leave your current job?
- What would your coworkers say about you?
- How would you describe yourself to your prior mentees?
- How did your previous work experience help you prepare for this position?
- Can you describe your management style?
- What effect does this have on the way you train?
- How do you stay up to date on the most recent training techniques?
- Can you explain why anyone should recruit you?

Introspection- Mentee

- What do you think your greatest assets are?
- How can you build the necessary discipline to achieve your objectives in this field?

- What are the necessary abilities for you to advance quickly in your career?
- What are some things you wish you had done earlier in your career?
- How can you efficiently manage your time and set priorities?
- Have you ever experienced impostor syndrome?
- How did you manage to overcome it?
- Were there any difficulties in getting started in this field?
- What were some difficult decisions you had to make in order to get to where you are now in your career?
- Have you had any big setbacks in your business or career?
- How did you get back on your feet?
- What are some things you might have done differently in certain situations?
- What can I do to improve you handling of this situation?
- Do you have any recommendations for internet networking?
- What are some options for resolving this problem?
- Your boss and coworkers are unfairly treating me. Based on your experience, do you think you should relocate?
- How should you prepare for performance evaluations?
- Are you progressing throughout this mentorship?
- Am I moving forward in the correct direction?
- Am I following your advice correctly?
- Is there anything else you'd like to talk about?
- Do you have any suggestions for how we could strengthen our mentoring relationship?
- How can I improve my critical job skills?
- How can I remain competitive in my field?
- How can I put my strengths to use in my day-to-day work?1.
- Who should you communicate with in order to advance my career?
- How do you see my industry evolving over the next five years?
- How do you get started on changing careers?
- What can you do at work to integrate my hobbies or passions?

- What can you do to take a more proactive approach to my job path?
- How can you make my work more meaningful?
- What positive habits should you develop to help yourself concentrate on my career?
- Who are some of the leaders who inspire you?
- Do you have any leadership books to recommend?
- What methods do you use to keep your staff motivated?
- What characteristics do today's leaders lack?
- How do you keep growing and developing as a leader?
- What was your worst decision as a leader?
- What was the most difficult disagreement you ever had to deal with?
- What was your most significant leadership risk?
- As a leader, what was your proudest achievement?
- What are your present leadership objectives?
- What was your worst decision as a leader?
- As a leader, what was your proudest achievement?
- What are your present leadership objectives?
- What do you like best about becoming an entrepreneur?
- What is the most difficult aspect of it?
- What are some blunders you wish you hadn't made?
- What recommendations would you provide to a first-time business owner?
- How do you come up with and finalise company concepts?
- What are the most common blunders made by first-time entrepreneurs?
- How do you want to expand your company or entrepreneurial mindset?
- What was the most difficult part of your company's journey?
- How did you get through it?
- Do you agree or disagree with any common entrepreneurship advice? Why?
- Have you ever made a mistake and felt like you'd failed? How did you get back on your feet?

- How did you learn to be comfortable with taking risks?
- Tell me about a recent business setback.How did you get back on your feet?
- Take a five-year look back.Did you ever see yourself in the position you're in now?
- Have you ever applied for and gotten a job that you weren't 100% qualified for? How did you go about it?
- What do you wish you had known before taking your first management position?
- What were the most difficult leadership skills to develop?
- Can you tell me about a time when you worked for a supervisor who was difficult?
- What steps did you take to deal with the situation?
- What is the most useful leadership lesson you've learnt, and how has it helped you?
- How did you hone your ability to talk so eloquently in front of groups?
- With whom do you need to align in order to succeed in this organization?
- Your manager said that you should be more strategic. What exactly does that imply?
- How can you communicate to my supervisor that I don't require micromanagement?
- How do you remain in touch with important influencers who don't work in the same workplace as me?
- What strategies have worked for you in gaining buy-in to execute a new program?
- Your performance evaluation is approaching. What kind of planning do you value the most from your employees?
- You may choose between two quite distinct job paths. Could anyone provide you with any advice to assist you in making a final decision?
- You are thinking about changing careers. What other sectors of the business do you think would be a good fit for?

- You've heard that doing a stretch assignment can help you advance in your job. What are the advantages and disadvantages?
- How do you perceived?
- To put it another way, what is your personal brand within our company?
- What do you think my strengths are?
- What do you think your blind spots are, and how can you improve them? What does leadership think of you?
- When you're not in the room, what do others say about you?
- Could you please give me some pointers on how can you improve your executive presence?
- In your day-to-day conversation, do you come across as strategic or tactical? When you email your employer weekly status updates, are you perceived as high-maintenance?
- What could you have done better to make your point more clear?
- How did you fare at the last meeting when you gave a presentation?
- Were your communication style appropriate for the message you wanted to convey?
- What can you do to become a more forceful negotiator?
- Is it possible to role-play asking for a raise or promotion?
- How can you improve my management of personnel who don't report to me? Do you have any quick re-energizing ideas for a tired team?
- Do you have a book or resource that you can recommend for dealing with uncomfortable conversations?
- Do you have any tips for coping with nerves while speaking in front of a group?
- What are some of the secrets to achieving success?
- What is a decent project management process or tool for tracking team commitments?
- Do you have a framework for long-term visioning and strategic planning that you use?

- What new talents do you require to advance?
- What can I do to become a more forceful negotiator?
- Is it possible to role-play asking for a raise or promotion?
- How can you improve my management of personnel who don't report to you? Do you have any quick re-energizing ideas for a tired team?
- Do you have a book or resource that you can recommend for dealing with uncomfortable conversations?
- Do you have any tips for coping with nerves while speaking in front of a group?
- What are some of the secrets to achieving success?
- What is a decent project management process or tool for tracking team commitments?
- Do you have a framework for long-term visioning and strategic planning that you use?
- What new talents do you require to advance?

"Nobody cares how much you know until they know how much you care." - Theodore Roosevelt

Finding And Benefiting From A Mentor

To find a mentor once you've determined the path you want to take in your career and defined your development areas. And believe you can all instinctively grasp why it matters when it comes to job advancement. In my own experience, mentors have aided me in taking more considered chances. They've been supportive and listened to me while I considered quitting politics to establish my own career advisory firm. They've assisted me in disseminating information about my programs and services, as well as assisting me in overcoming roadblocks. I would never have imagined who in my network would have served as the finest mentors of my whole career if I had to guess. Some of my closest mentors appear to have nothing in common with me at first glance, but they've been invaluable sounding boards as I've navigated my own professional changes. It's difficult to predict who will be your best mentor. To begin, think about what you want to learn. Find out where the people who know about it are and go meet them. Reach out to people you like and wish to mimic or who have experience in areas related to the abilities you want to develop. When it comes to professional admiration, who you admire reflects your ideals, so trust your gut and listen to your heart if you find yourself drooling over someone else's work. So, while looking for a mentor, consider the following factors: Your personal growth goals. If you need to learn how to sell yourself on social media, look for someone who has already done so successfully. As part of our mentoring relationship, you'll be delving into and covering a wide range of topics, so I want you to complete your homework before we meet for the first time. So just start by telling them exactly what you're looking for. Tell them why you picked them, what you hope to get out of the mentoring relationship, and then seal the deal. Prepare to discuss your previous job experience and the responsibilities you've held.

Who Should Be Your Mentor?

It all had to do with mentors who helped motivate me when I had just graduated from university and was unsure how to make the most of my life. It's advantageous to have powerful allies. They can assist with mentoring and sponsorship, which entails making contacts and opening doors. When it came to reaching out and interacting with possible mentors, one of my friends whom I picked as my mentor opened doors for me, but I felt a significant power imbalance at the time. Mentorship, I had no idea, is extremely helpful to both sides. You may be asking yourself, what does a mentor have to gain? I'll address your most pressing mentorship issues so you may provide a helping hand and raise people while you advance in your profession. I'm pleased to be both a mentor and a mentee these days. The majority of conventional mentorships involve a senior employee mentoring a group of junior colleagues. Mentors, on the other hand, do not have to be more senior than the people they guide. The most important thing is that mentors have experience from which others might benefit.

Connecting With A Mentor

In other words, mentors and proteges who regard themselves as deeply and meaningfully similar to one another have a high degree of like and chemistry with each other. So, based on this research, here are three strategies to assist you in developing chemistry with your mentee. To begin, consider surface-level similarities. Consider how good it feels to attend a networking event and discover you have something in common with someone. In a professional situation, I strongly advise you to use LinkedIn as a tool to develop surface-level commonality. So look over each other's profiles and see what you have in common on the surface. Look for commonalities on a deeper level. Using the Relationship Development Plan is a fantastic place to start. This is included in the exercise files and can assist you in probing for deep parallels in what truly counts, such as personalities, values, and aspirations.Be empathetically contagious.Emotions are very infectious, according to research. Remember that while chemistry may appear to be magical, it is something that can be improved if you are willing to work on it. People who have mentors receive significant professional rewards, such as higher income, promotions, and overall job satisfaction. However, I believe that learning how to connect with a mentor may also be a life hack for personal achievement. Life continues to present us with new problems that force us to change our identities and learn new abilities. When you need to learn something new, you may overcome problems more readily if you can establish a new team of mentors. I'll walk you through four stages when choosing a mentor. First and foremost, know that you believe in yourself. Before you can connect with a mentor, you must first understand who you are and what you want from a mentor. You must also understand what you can give a mentor and think that you are deserving of one. I've included an exercise file to help you figure out what you want to give a mentor. Mentorship, appreciation, passion, friendship, and exposure to new ideas have all benefited from an expanded network. Make a list of the top three things you feel you can give a mentor. Believe that you have a lot to contribute, even if it's simply your heartfelt gratitude.

Consider who you should contact. Consider someone you like and would like to connect with, or recollect your aims and desires. Don't censor yourself when you're reflecting. True, you may not be able to hire a company's top executive straight away. However, perhaps you can meet with them once and they can introduce you to someone who can become your mentor. Finally, look for possible mentors.

Mentor- Mentee Matching Goal

A mentoring program's strength can be attributed to its ability to match mentors and mentees. However, if you try to conduct the matching manually, it might be a significant challenge. One of the most significant advantages of employing mentoring software is its capacity to generate matches in a matter of minutes. Mentoring software features algorithms that discover excellent matches based on information gathered from participants as well as the mentor program management. Once you've found a solid match, give the mentoring every chance to succeed by teaching both the mentor and the mentee about their expectations and how to get the most out of the mentorship. Participants may be required to attend seminars or training sessions on communication strategies. Participants may be required to attend seminars or training sessions on communication strategies and leadership abilities. Every excellent mentoring program should ask its participants for feedback. This allows you to see which aspects of the application are operating effectively and which may need to be changed. Feedback can take numerous forms, such as an interview after the mentee completes the mentorship, or it might simply be a questionnaire that participants fill out after the experience. It makes no difference how you obtain the feedback; what matters is what you do with it. There will be occasions when one of the participants does not believe it is effective. At this stage, an administrator can assist in defining and resolving the issue, which may entail dissolving the match and forming a new one. Although tracking communication may appear to be a time-consuming chore, it will be made easier if you use a mentoring software tool. Program administrators can track emails and meetings using mentoring software. It can also make it easier to remain in touch with participants. Hayley Romer is one of the world's busiest individuals. She is not only the publisher of The Atlantic, but she also works in a highly competitive business that is constantly evolving. Nonetheless, she took time out many times a month to have lunch or breakfast with colleagues from all throughout the company. Because her staff are also customers, she gets a sense of what's going on in the marketplace when she does that. Two, she's keeping tabs on how her staff are feeling and what difficulties or possibilities exist in the talent dynamics.

Summing Up

Start by carefully listening and asking plenty of questions to gain a feel for your mentee's overall goals. Mentoring software can assist in tracking objectives so that mentees can see how far they have progressed. Some of my closest mentors have been invaluable sounding boards as I've navigated my own professional changes. If you need to learn how to sell yourself on social media, look for someone who has already done so successfully. Mentors do not have to be more senior than the people they guide. I strongly advise you to use LinkedIn as a tool to develop surface-level commonality. People who have mentors receive significant professional rewards, such as higher income and promotion. I believe that learning how to connect with a mentor may also be a life hack for personal achievement. Before you can connect with a mentor, you must first understand who you are and what you want. Consider someone you like and would like to connect with, or recollect your aims and desires. Make a list of the top three things you feel you can give a mentor.

CHAPTER EIGHT

NEWER GENERATION NEWER APPROACHES

"A small amount of time invested on your part to share your expertise can open up a new world for someone else."

-Mark Zuckerberg

Finding , understand that while the distinctions are essential, the commonalities outweigh them. In the workplace, everyone has the same basic needs: stability, inclusion, and recognition. With a predicted global talent shortfall of 85.2 million by 2030, leaders must invest in working settings that address common values while also building respect for differences. Mentorship can be targeted to specific individuals with a strong culture in place. Generation X. Millennials Generation Z is the next generation. The fact that the labour force is made up of five generations for the first time has gotten a lot of attention.

Consider how training and support may be integrated into the mentoring process to make it more approachable and available to everybody. Provide your staff with relationship-building strategies and methods that they may apply, regardless of their generation. By demystifying the mentoring process and overcoming generational preconceptions, they will be able to perceive one another as individuals rather than caricatures. It may appear to be entertaining to indulge in tribalism and determine where individuals belong based on arbitrary variables such as generation, but it can actually cause more harm than good. It's past time for us to stop categorising people and start recognising them as individuals who contribute to our work and life.

If you're in charge of a team in today's workplace, you're probably dealing with numerous generations—often up to four! As the workplace experiences a significant demographic shift, multigenerational management has become a hot issue in recent months. The most challenging question remains: how can a multigenerational leader get the benefits of generational diversity while minimising the costs? Employees in a multigenerational workplace are more likely to instinctively engage with those in their own age group, forming *"generational cliques,"* rather than genuine friendships with others on the team who are different from them.This is a common misunderstanding.

#Myth: Younger employees are entitled and lazy, whereas older employees are lethargic and unwilling to learn new skills. The development of your team will be harmed by these generational stereotypes. The truth is that every generation on your team has something valuable to offer the team and the company as a whole.

Your organization is poised for increased innovation and problem-solving by lowering generational conflict, enabling understanding and open communication, and improving team growth.A multigenerational mentoring program can help you identify and share such abilities with others in your team. Multigenerational mentorship overcomes this obstacle by enabling employees of all ages and generations to form deeper bonds with one another. It also aids in the improvement of their interpersonal communication. Understanding others' viewpoints, values, and experiences, as well as better communication, are the keys to avoiding workplace conflict and encouraging greater team development and innovation. Mentoring can be done in a variety of ways, including one-on-one, reverse mentoring, group mentoring, and more. Don't limit your mentoring possibilities based on your assumptions about the preferences of different generations. Well, millennials prefer collaborative learning, so we'll provide group mentoring to them, and Gen Z wants to demonstrate their value to the organization, so we'll provide reverse mentoring to them. Instead of limiting people's options, give them a variety of options so they can choose for themselves whatever type of mentoring they wish to use. For almost a decade, the Baby Boomers, Gen X, and Gen Y/Millennials have collaborated and competed for power and influence. Gen Z those born after 1995 is now entering the workforce and poised to make an impact. Some people prefer face-to-face meetings, while others prefer email. Others choose to communicate via text, video chat, or over the phone. If you believe generational stereotypes, you might believe that Gen X prefers email to video chatting. However, as technology becomes more widespread, making assumptions is risky. Allow people to make their own decisions about how they communicate with their mentees/mentors instead. Give them complete control over the connection. Despite the fact that different generations have had diverse life experiences, we all have more in common than we know.Most of us would benefit from having a mentor who could assist us at work and serve as a guide and sounding board as we progress in our careers. Mentoring is also a natural action in which we all participate without even realising it. Whether we want to be mentored to acquire a new skill, advance in our careers, or gain a new perspective, we all want to improve ourselves. In reality, the Pew Research Center amended their millennial age range definition in March 2018 to include these post-Millennial Gen Zs. The book Modern Mentoring by Randy Emelo takes into account these new generational definitions and perspectives on mentoring. Millennials can attest to how aggravating and inconvenient this is as they fight generational stereotypes like being entitled, lazy, and self-absorbed. Instead of looking at different generations and deciding on a mentoring method based on prejudices, consider the following universal suggestions for making mentoring more approachable and accessible to everyone in your organization:

According to a Gallup poll, 34% of American workers are engaged, and 70% of team engagement is directly tied to the manager or team leader's quality, implying that organizations that establish more caring workplace environments have a better success rate than those that do not. According to a Deloitte survey, millennials want mentorship in the workplace and believe they are more useful when someone invests in their leadership skills. They are also more likely to stay with a company for more than five years if it offers mentoring programs, according to the study. For the first time in history, managers face the enormous burden of understanding and guiding four generations in the workplace. In order to effectively manage the workforce, it is necessary to understand each generation and the variations between them. In today's business world, executives must employ techniques to effectively communicate and bridge generations in order to successfully manage a diverse workforce spanning many years. For the younger generations, connection is essential. Millennials and Generation Z, who are just starting out in the workforce, communicate in a different way than previous generations. While their communication styles differ and have practical benefits, they lose touch with one another in the process. Training younger generations to spend face-to-face time with other team members - a benefit that Gen Z employees value - and to invest in the professional growth of their peers and colleagues by spending significant one-on-one time will be beneficial to the success of your company and them as they progress in their careers.

Mentoring Gen Z Statistics:

- 76% of Gen Z see learning as the key to their advancement in their careers & 83% of Gen Z want to learn skills to perform better in their current position.
- 21% of Gen Z want their boss to have 'mentoring ability
- 73% of Gen Z would like to be taught one on one
- 77% of Gen Z said that a company's level of diversity affects their decision to work there
- 87% of Gen Z wants a job where they are able to learn a lot
- 82% say it is important that their supervisor helps them establish performance goals

- 83% of Gen Z wants their supervisors to care about their life

According to a Robert Half study, open lines of communication, lots of face-to-face time, and mentoring are among the top attributes of a firm sought by Gen Z, the generation after millennials. While numerous types of mentoring exist, such as one-on-one mentoring and reverse mentoring, in which junior employees mentor their superiors on a number of cultural subjects, nurturing talent has long-term benefits that can be quantified in a variety of ways. Here are a few of the most compelling reasons why becoming a mentor and fostering talent is so vital to running a successful company. There is a lot of passion among young entrepreneurs, and they have high ambitions. While the excitement over what Gen Z wants and expects in the workplace is finally dying down, talk about the next generation is just getting started. Get ready, because Gen Alpha, those born between early 2010 and mid 2020, is on its way. Mentors provide more than just guidance and brainstorming assistance; they also serve as confidants with whom you can share your concerns. They'll listen to you, help you figure out what's upsetting you, and support you as you brainstorm solutions together. Reverse mentorship frequently conjures up images of a tech-savvy recent college graduate sitting down with a practically retired employee and teaching them how to traverse ever-changing devices and technology. While previous generations learned how to be more flexible and efficient with technology, Gen Y and Gen Z have access to some of the top executives who are normally unavailable to entry-level employees. Gen X and Gen Y develop their networks and become more visible to executive leaders who are interested in cultivating high-potential employees who may be called upon to continue a legacy where solid relationships are built.

Mentoring Millennials Statistics:

- 79% of millennials see mentoring as crucial to their career success

- But 63% of millennials say their leadership skills are not being fully developed
- 49% of millennials would, if they had a choice, quit their current jobs in the next two years and millennials will comprise more than 75% of the workforce by 2025
- 91% of Millennials consider the potential for career progression as a top priority when choosing a new job
- 53% of Millennials have been disappointed by a lack of personal development training when starting a new job
- Less than 50% of Millennials say they've had opportunities at work to learn and grow within the past year
- 93% of millennials find skill development crucial for their career

A pilot program of reverse mentoring is addressing experience gaps at Burson-Marsteller, a public relations and communications firm with offices in 85 countries. The company provided training for both Millennial mentors and their older mentees, creating confidentiality guidelines. While studies, experts, and managers disagree about the basic motivational factors and values-based differences between generations, one conclusion is unmistakable. The variations in experience, talents, and usage of technology are obvious when four (if not five) generations work together in a company. 75% of millennials deem mentoring critical to their success, and they know that in order to stay relevant they need to take personal responsibility for their own learning. If your company hasn't yet experienced an invasion of Millennials (those born between 1980 and 2000), it will. Millennials (also known as Generation Y) will be more than 60% of the worldwide workforce by 2025. Millennials recognise that everyone has inherent value and, as a result, are open to learning from, well, everyone. A study conducted by the Inter-University Council of East Africa supported this observation. The study indicated that at least 60% of graduates from local universities are ill-equipped for the marketplace upon graduation. In addition, a study conducted by PWC showed that 80% of CEOs see lack of human capital as the biggest threat to growth of businesses. This large opportunity gap for college graduates who aren't yet ready or prepared to join the workforce keeps economies moving slowly. Keep in mind that while the disparities are significant, they are not insurmountable. Differences in communication style, technical competence, or organizational knowledge, on the other hand, may serve as the foundation for what an employee needs to learn. Look for cross-pollination chances in this situation. Combining expertise with rookies, technology with creativity, and rebels with process gurus is a winning combination. General Motors CEOMary Barra's career hasn't been shaped by just one or two mentors; instead, it's been influenced by a network of them. In a survey of 2,200 professionals from a variety of industries, they were asked about their beliefs, work conduct, and what they expected from their employers. We saw that Millennials wanted continuous feedback and were eager to succeed, but their expectations were not as lofty as many people believe. Working is viewed as an important component of life by Millennials, not as a distinct activity that must be "balanced" by it. As a result, people place a high value on finding a job that is personally rewarding. Yes, Millennials expect a lot from their employers, but they also expect a lot from themselves. Because there are so many of them, they've been working on their résumés since they were toddlers. Michael Bloomberg has achieved a lot of professional success as a wealthy businessman, an entrepreneur, and a former mayor of New York City. Bloomberg attributes much of his success to the late William R. Salomon, managing partner of the former financial house Salomon Brothers, where he began his career as a trader. Bloomberg writes. *"He taught by leading, and he led by example. On most mornings, he'd be the first one in the office. He was a good listener, but he didn't manage by consensus. He was his own man, he made his own decisions, and he didn't look back."* Shark Tank's Robert Herjavec's most memorable moment with a mentor was completely unplanned. He was having a conversation with his then-boss, Warner Avis, the founder of Avis Rent a Car. Avis led Herjavec to an office window and, pointing to a hot-dog vendor down below,

He *"told me that I was acting like the vendor—pushing product, and doing all the work to make a living,"* Herjavec writes. *"He followed that statement with, 'You need to be the guy supplying the dogs to all the vendors if you ever want to scale."*

Choosing The Best Option Of Mentoring

Group mentoring: The mentees gain from working with a more senior mentor, but they also get the added benefit of working with and being nurtured by their peers, which aligns with the Millennial mindset.

Situational mentoring. The aim is defined, and the mentoring relationship is short-term, ending when the goal is met. For example, if the mentee wishes to brush up on her sales call manners, she could seek advice and comments from one of the office's senior sales reps.

"It was a stroke of luck that he was there." He was my best mentor, and I used to walk into his office and say things like, "J (RD), I wish this had occurred 10 years ago. We had such a beautiful relationship." He was like a father and a brother to him, and he replied, "Not enough has been spoken about that."

You might be wondering if a person can participate in situational mentoring, group mentoring, and traditional one-on-one mentoring all at once. Yes, and this "tri-brid" concept may appeal to Millennials since it satisfies their desire for regular learning and feedback.

Hybrid Mentoring Programs: Develop mentoring programs that may be used by workers of all ages and stages of their careers. Programs should be as global as feasible, encouraging information sharing and interaction between mentors and mentees all around the world. Face-to-face, online, experiential learning, and digital platforms (e.g., Slack, What's App, Skype, Zoom, etc.) should all be used to provide program material.

Traditional mentoring: It is still relevant and meaningful, especially to those "other" generations that still make up the workforce Gen X and Boomers. It's still relevant and meaningful, especially to the "other" generations in the workforce Gen X and Boomers. Allow your employees to select the flavors that best suit them.And don't be shocked if some of the new products appeal to the older generations couldn't we all benefit from some situational mentorship now and then?. Whenever everybody else thinks your idea is absolutely barmy, it could actually prove to be a stroke of genius. Richard Branson.He credits his oddball Uncle Jim with teaching him an important lesson: "*When everyone else thinks your idea is crazy, that may be a sign you're really onto something. Uncle Jim's habit of eating grass was widely mocked in the army, until it earned him a role as. "*

Reverse Mentoring: Many years ago, a mentor taught me this notion. As a mentee, this is an excellent chance to return some of your mentor's valuable advice and or assistance. This is a terrific chance for mentors who aren't technologically aware to learn about and get a "crash course" on some of the latest digital tools and apps. For example, I frequently provide advice on how to improve my mentors' digital presence (e.g., blogging, social networking, etc.) as well as digital tools to assist them in maintaining their digital presence.

Newer Approaches & Fundamental Truth

- Learn directly from a mentor—a kind elder sibling, a guardian angel instructor, an office associate or senior who will take you under their wing, or a wise parent.
- Building and operating a business isn't rocket science, but it does include making practical tradeoffs, cultivating strong relationships, and taking calculated risks, all of which can be assisted by a one-on-one mentor.
- Mentorship serves as a fourth wheel in the growth of managers, as well as in business and life experience and formal education. Nothing can ever replace a mentor passing on hard-won knowledge to a mentee.
- Employee development can be facilitated by a formal mentorship program, which allows employees to gain critical skills and obtain valuable insights from more experienced peers. Gaps are filled by these meaningful encounters.

- Mentorship should be a part of your company's culture on a long-term basis. Mentorship is also a crucial component of good management teams, ensuring the company's overall success.
- In today's internet world, mentoring has evolved from the traditional one-on-one method to encompass more flexible models such as virtual mentoring and group mentoring.
- Provide your staff with helpful hints for making their interactions successful. People can perceive one another as distinct human beings rather than oversimplified caricatures by demystifying the mentoring process and assisting them to see past generational prejudices.
- Individuals from different generations are paired for the purpose of mutual learning and growth in cross-generational mentorship. Employees can build a bridge by forming mentorship relationships in which several generations share their experiences, skills, and expertise. The generational and talent gaps that exist between these two groups will be bridged by this bridge.
- Organizations can lessen the generational gap/divide and identify strategies to turn stereotypes into active learning opportunities by using reverse mentorship and frequent collaboration for change.
- Rather than limiting the types of mentoring available, provide people with a wide range of possibilities so they can choose what type of mentoring they want.
- Mentors should provide talented people the freedom to explore and make decisions outside of their comfort zones. Encourage mentees to see these events as part of their path, even if they aren't successful.
- Mentorship is frequently recommended as a strategy to break down organizational silos, promote collaboration, and speed knowledge transfer. However, mentorship is often a top-down, one-way method of development.
- Individuals from different generations are paired for the purpose of mutual learning and growth in cross-generational

mentorship. Employees can build a bridge by forming mentorship relationships in which several generations share their experiences, skills, and expertise. The generational and talent gaps that exist between these two groups will be bridged by this bridge.

- Reverse mentoring, on the other hand, can create a healthy two-way connection in which both sides profit from the exchange and rely on one another's experiences and natural abilities. Younger generations are partnered with older generations in a reverse mentorship program, and both sides are required to contribute their knowledge to ensure that all employees are well-rounded.
- Mentoring programs should last longer than a week or a month. Rather, they complete the circle when previous trainees become mentors. Motivate future leaders to see potential in their colleagues or new personnel. To initiate a new cycle of learning transfer and leadership continuity, pair them with suitable mentors.
- Taking on difficult jobs also helps trainees develop important skills that will help them become more resilient and innovative leaders. The mentorship program relies heavily on effective communication. In addition to providing expert guidance, mentors can assist prospective leaders by publicly expressing their support. Mentees are then given the option to give comments on how they feel about their performance, which is especially important following a difficult job. A mentee, for example, may have an inventive solution that helps improve workflow or build new business programs.
- Both mentor and mentee put in a lot of time and effort into the program and their relationships, and it's well worth it.
- Mentors' efforts are recognised with a thank you note or a tribute, while incentives and promotions keep future leaders engaged. You can also express your gratitude by awarding certificates or plaques.

- If you want to make mentoring easy for your employees, they can also use the software to set relationship goals and track their progress toward them.
- A constructive relationship is ensured when the mentor and mentee characteristics are matched, resulting in a successful mentoring program. Mentoring sessions not only teach future leaders but also expose them to other aspects of the business.Future leaders can learn to appreciate varied jobs by rotating assignments.
- Managers can employ reverse mentoring to break down preconceptions and misconceptions by having younger workers mentor members of older generational groups. Employees can find a common ground to share their knowledge by having people from various age groups mentor one another. This allows Millennials to give their knowledge of technology and marketing, while the Silent and Baby Boomer generations have years of expertise to share, such as professional attire recommendations.
- Without mentors, neither the world's innovations nor the mentees' capacity to invest in themselves in their creations would have been possible. On the other hand, if the mentor is stressed, they can use it as material for a learning activity for their mentee. Because they're friends who trust each other's abilities and good judgement more than most, both the mentor and the mentee benefit from the relationship's stress-relieving power.
- When you can effectively manage a multigenerational workforce, your company will benefit from increased innovation, better cooperation and problem-solving, more engaged employees, and happier consumers. A multigenerational mentorship program is a simple modification that may have a significant influence on your team, corporate culture, and financial results.

Even the most successful CEOs and business leaders admit that they had a mentor who made all the difference along the road. *Indeed, 86 percent of the 1,348 CEOs polled in the August 2020 Vistage CEO Confidence Index survey believed that mentors were an important component of their professional success. 62% of CEOs said they were currently mentoring someone professionally.*

"As we look ahead into the next century, leaders will be those who empower others." – Bill Gates

Gates' ability to "explain things that are complex and put them in a simple form so that people may comprehend and profit from all of his expertise" allowed him to reach his full potential and defy the label of "high school dropout." As is often the case, billionaire Michael Bloomberg came from humble beginnings, and he, too, owes his success to a mentor who instilled in him the ideals and ideas that would lead to such a prosperous career.

"If you ask any successful businessperson, they will always (say they) have had a great mentor at some point along the road." – Richard Branson

Richard Branson recognises the value of mentorship. During his attempt to get Virgin Atlantic off the ground, Branson sought advice from British airline entrepreneur Sir Freddie Laker. At the outset, "it's always wonderful to have a helping hand." Branson wrote in the British daily The Sun. Without Sir Freddie Laker's guidance, I would not have progressed in the airline sector.

"Understandably, there's a lot of ego, nervous energy, and parental pride involved, especially with one-or two-person start-ups... Going it alone is admirable, but it's also a risky and incorrect strategy for taking on the world. " - Richard Branson

Cross-gender & Women In Mentorship

When we talk about cross-gender mentorship, I know it may seem like we're walking through a minefield because we're afraid of saying the wrong thing or unwittingly causing events. My mentorship study, on the other hand, demonstrates unequivocally that having a network of diverse sorts of individuals, including gender diversity, is beneficial to both men and women. In this video, I'll give you tips on how to make your cross-gender relationships succeed. First, admit to yourself and your mentor that gender disparities matter in the relationship and in other people's impressions.I have addressed the significance of cross-gender mentorship connections. Choose your mentoring activities with caution, and maybe in a different way in cross-gender interactions. You are the one who determines your boundaries and what you are comfortable with. Most cross-gender partnerships are completely professional. But keep in mind that controlling other people's perceptions is just as crucial as managing your own.

According to studies, Millennials and Generation Z are twice as likely as older generations to be disengaged at work. Employees who are more engaged produce higher-quality work. As a result, employee engagement is critical, especially as the younger workforce continues to rise. With an average of 5,900 new retirees per year, the baby boomer group is rapidly ageing. Mentorship can boost employee engagement and help them do better work. This is especially true when it comes to cross-generational mentorship, as the older generations are more involved. Combining them with younger generations will increase their engagement, resulting in a better firm and increased production. Employee retention, particularly among millennials, might be boosted by mentorship programs. Mentorees from the younger generation will be able to discuss their goals and ideas with someone who has walked in their footsteps.

Mentoring for Diversity Statistics:

- Mentoring programs boosted minority representation at the management level from 9% to 24%
- As well as promotion and retention rates for minorities and women from 15% to 38% as compared to non-mentored employees
- Women are more likely to have a mentor than men – 54% vs 48%
- 38% of female employees (in companies that have at least 30% women on their board) who have exposure to senior mentors

believe they will make it to the board themselves, compared with 21% of women from companies under 30% target

Indra Nooyi, CEO of PepsiCo, looks for mentors in all facets of her life: "*I wouldn't be here today if I hadn't had mentors.*" I'm a result of excellent mentoring and coaching... Coaches or mentors are really valuable. She attributes her ability to break through glass ceilings in business to the coaching she received from others. Sheryl Sandberg, the chief operating officer of Facebook, is widely regarded as one of the most powerful women in business today. She, like most successful people, sought the advice of mentors at various points in her career. Larry Summers, Sandberg's former college professor, had a critical role in her career as both a mentor and a sponsor. Women have never required more help than they do today, especially since the outbreak of the epidemic. During the epidemic, McKinsey research indicated that women were 1.8 times more likely than males to lose their employment. Despite accounting for 39% of worldwide employment, women were responsible for 54% of job losses.

In the workplace, the boardroom, and at the head of the table, women are priceless resources. According to various research, firms with more gender diversity are more lucrative. Women have high emotional intelligence. Emotional intelligence, or the ability to sense, manage, and analyse emotions, is an important leadership trait. Leaders with strong emotional intelligence can build a fantastic environment and get the most out of their staff. This is a characteristic that women have more naturally than men. They understand the importance of work-life balance in fostering a positive workplace culture: Women understand the importance of work-life balance in fostering a positive workplace culture.They are wonderful leaders because they are concerned about the well-being of their staff, which includes their own. They are excellent leaders because they are concerned about their colleagues' well-being, including their work-life balance. With a personal request or a delicate subject, approaching a female leader is easier.

Furthermore, during the epidemic, women's job hours were drastically decreased, and they spent more time on domestic responsibilities and child care, according to another study. In today's workplace, women are more susceptible. When asked about their professional paths, most successful entrepreneurs attribute their success to a mentor or mentors. Women can negotiate in high-stakes scenarios because they have the following qualities: According to research, women are more adept at closing agreements than men. According to the New York Times, female senators are better at working with people who have opposing viewpoints to get things done than their male colleagues. No one learns in a vacuum, and the men and women who can soak up the wisdom of others – and then pay it forward by becoming mentors themselves when the time comes – are the ones who stand out. As a result, formal mentorship—particularly women mentoring other women—can be beneficial to them.In today's workplace, there is a significant mentoring gap for women. SHRM polled 318 businesswomen from 19 different countries and 30 different industries. They discovered that while 63 percent of women had never had a formal mentor, 67 percent considered mentorship to be extremely essential in advancing and growing their professions. There is a mentoring gap for women. To empower women and create a diverse workforce, businesses require organised mentorship programs. According to a McKinsey report, 72 percent of respondents feel there is a significant link between a diverse workforce, women, and financial success. With an average of 5,000 new baby boomers exiting the workforce every day, the baby boomer generation is rapidly retiring. While at a slower pace than their predecessors, this generation is nonetheless quitting their companies at a steady pace. This means that organizations must assist boomers in passing on their expertise to younger generations before they pass away. Through cross-generational mentorship, high-potential employees can become mentees of leadership mentors. This combination is perfect for developing the succession pipeline for future leadership roles. A cohesive multi-generational workforce may appear unattainable; however, it provides unrivalled benefits to companies with the vision and values to reap the benefits of this unique form of diversity.The key to success is mentoring that focuses on individual abilities. Mentorship allows women to improve their leadership abilities and expand their professional networks both within and outside of business. It increases their confidence, allowing them to speak up in meetings and apply for leadership roles within the firm. Women are also hesitant to speak up for themselves, which is an important leadership trait. Mentorship encourages women to be more confident in their own skin as self-advocates, allowing them to ask questions and learn from their errors.

Summing Up

Leaders must invest in working settings that address common values while building respect for differences. Every employee has something valuable to offer the team and the company as a whole. A multigenerational mentoring program can help you identify and share such abilities with others in your team. Mentoring can be done in a variety of ways, including one-on-one and reverse mentoring. Don't limit your options based on assumptions about the preferences of different generations. Executives must employ techniques to effectively communicate and bridge generations in order to successfully manage a diverse workforce spanning many years. Instead of looking at different generations and deciding on a mentoring method based on prejudices, consider the following suggestions for making mentoring more approachable and accessible. Open lines of communication, face-to-face time, and mentoring are top attributes sought by Gen Z. Nurturing talent has long-term benefits that can be quantified in a variety of ways. Mentorship serves as a fourth wheel in the growth of managers, as well as in business and life experience. In today's internet world, mentoring has evolved from the traditional one-on-one model to more flexible models such as virtual mentoring and group mentoring. Managers can employ reverse mentoring to break down preconceptions and misconceptions. A multigenerational mentorship program is a simple modification that may have a significant influence on your team, corporate culture, and financial results. This allows Millennials to share their knowledge of technology and marketing, while the silent and baby boomer generations share years of expertise. Leaders with strong emotional intelligence can build a fantastic environment and get the most out of their staff. Women understand the importance of work-life balance in fostering a positive workplace culture. With a personal request or a delicate subject, approaching a female leader is easier. There is a significant mentoring gap for women in the workplace. To empower women and create a diverse workforce, businesses require organised mentorship programs.

CHAPTER NINE

TECHNOLOGICAL ADVANCEMENT IN MENTORSHIP

"My job is not to be easy on people. My job is to take these great people we have and to push them and make them even better."
-Steve Jobs

Mentoring is commonly regarded as one of the most effective and influential methods for assisting a person in gaining experience, learning new skills, developing, and eventually growing in their profession. As a result, mentoring is frequently employed as a tactic in businesses of all sizes. Mentoring is also gaining popularity, with more and more companies offering it to their employees as a method to improve employee engagement, knowledge exchange, and retention. It has, however, always been a difficult technique to put into practise. From video conferencing platforms (e.g., Zoom, Google Hangouts) to online collaboration tools (e.g., Slack, Microsoft Teams), technology has increased the flexibility with which mentors and mentees can connect and stay connected, just as it has in our businesses, schools, and society at large. It is not an exaggeration to argue that "the existing structure of society today" is heavily reliant on technology and everything that it brings with it. Learning is at the forefront, as it has always been. Sure, the world's top corporations are consumer success stories-mobile phones, electronic products, e-commerce, and so on. A strong mentorship program is a smart way to link your employees' personal goals with the goals of your company. Your workplace culture will thrive if those two interests are aligned. We saw a global epidemic that shut down practically every business for at least part of the year, with the majority of people having to work from home if they were lucky enough to save their employment at all. Technology enablement to facilitate employee communication is in higher demand than ever before. As a result, talent and opportunity marketplaces have become an essential tool for employees who still need to engage with managers and mentors throughout the organization's ecosystem. Progressive companies are using technology, such as artificial intelligence (AI), to build talent marketplaces that focus on employee connectivity and have a big impact on workplace transformation. Overall, this empowers potential employees by giving them more access to open employment and project opportunities, as well as increasing their capacity to connect with potential mentors, career routes, and the tools they'll need to advance their careers. According to a study, the main reason for two out of three fresh Singaporean graduates quitting their first job in less than a year was a desire for more professional progress rather than a higher income. Employees are less likely to become stagnant or disengaged at work if they continue to learn and grow alongside the company.

Technology, such as artificial intelligence (AI), is being used by forward-thinking companies to achieve their goals. Despite employee engagement programs, about 85 percent of employees worldwide are disengaged at work, according to Gallup's State of the Global Workplace 20212 survey. As a result, in a good mentoring program, making an authentic connection is crucial. Employers can use new technologies and trends to complement and expand traditional mentoring programs as the workplace advances. Mentorship isn't about pursuing the most senior executive in the hopes of advancing your career; it's about assessing the people in your life, at all levels, and determining who you connect with the best, who you respect and admire, and who is ready to interact with you – even through the internet. Great mentors recognise that offering constructive criticism or the correct tools empowers mentees to come up with their own solutions and paths ahead on their own. That's when you may have a significant impact on a person's professional and personal development. Statistical data reinforced the need for mentoring again and again.

71% of Fortune 500 companies offer mentoring programs. According to 79% of millennials *"Mentoring is critical to their success,"* .

75% of private-sector executives say *"Mentoring was crucial to my professional growth."*

Technology has recently gotten a bad rap for interfering with interpersonal connections and communication. At this point, the stereotype of the technophobic boomer resenting millennials for texting or emailing rather than picking up the phone is a tired and inaccurate one. With individuals spending an average of 11 hours per day in front of a computer, it's difficult to believe that workplace connections aren't being sacrificed in the sake of efficiency. Organizations have been increasingly reliant on technology to communicate rather than face-to-face meetings in order to save money and time on trip expenditures. However, successful mentoring programs have long been a challenge for businesses. Many organizations have embraced new technology in recent years that Homer could never have anticipated. Mentorlink, eMentorConnect, Mentorloop, MentorcliQ, MentorCloud, and Chronus are examples of platforms that support mentor-mentee matching, goal-setting, guided dialogues, and useful resources, as well as dashboards and reporting options for tracking engagement and success. Ellen, a powerful artificial-intelligence.

Technoligical Advancement In Mentorship

Technology enablement to facilitate employee communication is in higher demand than ever before. Progressive companies are using technology, such as artificial intelligence (AI), to build talent marketplaces that focus on employee connectivity and have a big impact on workplace transformation. Overall, this empowers potential employees by giving them more access to open employment and project opportunities, as well as increasing their capacity to connect with potential mentors, career routes, and the tools they'll need to advance their careers. According to a study, the main reason for two out of three fresh Singaporean graduates quitting their first job in less than a year was a desire for more professional progress rather than a higher income. Employees are less likely to become stagnant or disengaged at work if they continue to learn and grow alongside the company. Technology, such as artificial intelligence (AI), is being used by forward-thinking companies to achieve their goals. Despite employee engagement programs, about 85 percent of employees worldwide are disengaged at work, according to Gallup's State of the Global Workplace 2021survey. As a result, in a good mentoring program, making an authentic connection is crucial. Employers can use new technologies and trends to complement and expand traditional mentoring programs as the workplace advances. As more businesses use virtual communication tools and platforms, some may choose to conduct online mentorship sessions. Mentors may ask mentees who have been identified as having leadership potential to join in on virtual meetings, which is a less intrusive option than bringing in a new face to physical meetings.

Mentorship During Pandemic Situation

Human connection is more crucial than ever in these exceptional and uncertain times. This is compounded by the reality that most of our interactions will continue to take place on a virtual platform in the foreseeable future. You've been reminded of the value of mentorship. You must have done your utmost to bring people together, collaborate, and assist them to attain their full potential in the face of the COVID-19 epidemic. So, what does it take to be a good mentor, especially in today's age of social isolation? However, location isn't the only boundary that digital crosses; it also extends well beyond our personal circles. Today, the world is your oyster when it comes to mentorship. Few people are fortunate enough to meet Richard Branson, Jack Welch, or Hillary

Clinton for coffee, but that doesn't mean you can't use them as virtual mentors. You may learn from practically any expert in the world using LinkedIn, Twitter, Facebook, YouTube, and the other media at our disposal. Learn from their ideologies, techniques, biggest personal difficulties, accomplishments, and failures by following them. Pay attention to how these industry experts manage to stay on top of their game in a world that is getting quicker by the day. Though formal programs can be beneficial, the most successful and long-lasting mentorships are formed via true human connections. As the effect of COVID-19 has transformed industries and the job you perform on a daily basis, you may have discovered a new manager or colleague in your corner during the last several weeks. When mentees are able to be open and honest about their talents and ambitions—as well as their faults and anxieties—trust is developed. As COVID-19 spreads over the world, many offices are shuttering for staff safety as well as to comply with emergency directives from governing agencies. To say the least, there are a variety of reasons why a mentor and mentee might not be able to meet in person on a regular basis. It's an issue when a mentor and mentee can't meet on a regular basis, because consistency is essential for creating trust and chemistry in a mentoring relationship. When organizations use technology like online conferencing, mentors and mentees can continue to strengthen their connection even when in-person visits aren't possible. Professional mentoring connections might become increasingly important as a result of technological advancements. Of course, there are times when nothing beats plain old-fashioned face-to-face contact. Facial expressions, intonation, and other indicators that are lost in other communication modalities, such as written communication or chatting on the phone, are all present in face-to-face conversation. Face-to-face conversations also create trust more effectively than other types of communication. When people communicate in person, they feel more accountable to others. Face-to-face contact is preferable when dealing with some delicate problems. Employers with workplaces in regions with "stay-at-home" orders as a result of the Covid-19 issue, on the other hand, have no alternative but to communicate face to face. Many of us are scared, anxious, and overwhelmed as a result of the coronavirus pandemic. People are affected in a variety of ways, but worries about a loss of attention or productivity are typical. Mentors should constantly provide a support system for trainees and urge them to put their health first, especially during trying times like this. In a time of shuttered laboratories, depleted and exhausted healthcare colleagues, and social estrangement, we must redefine how we mentor. For online mentoring sessions and conversations, there are a plethora of excellent online video possibilities. Zoom is an excellent video conferencing application for one-on-one or larger group meetings. Another easy alternative is Google Meet, which is also accessible for free. Use your mentoring platform's in-app video conferencing facilities if they're accessible. If you don't have access to a computer, Skype and FaceTime are excellent online video solutions.

Benefits of Technology for Mentoring Programs

Because of technological advancements, mentoring programs may now flourish more than ever before. We've broken down communication barriers and decreased workloads thanks to technology. Not only that, but most talent development programs today incorporate technology.

- Mentoring programs are an excellent illustration of how technology may be beneficially integrated. Mentoring software includes several features, including the ability for mentors to connect with mentees all over the world. It's transforming the way organizations benefit from mentorship in the workplace for the betterment.
- You may have mentors and mentees who have less access to a laptop than a smartphone, or who just prefer the latter, depending on the mentoring program. If you're using mentoring software, look for one that includes a mobile mentoring app so that mentors and mentees can keep their mentoring connections

going even while they're on the road.

- Mentorship, like many other talent development programs, has numerous advantages. This is especially true with software-assisted mentoring. Here are a couple of instances: Using mentoring software, mentors and mentees no longer have to work in the same building.
- If a corporation starts a worldwide mentoring program, the mentee may be able to select a mentor from another continent. This implies that mentees will have a greater pool of mentors to pick from, with a wider range of specialities and knowledge.
- Mentoring software helps mentors and mentees communicate in the most effective way possible.
- Virtual mentoring allows employees to be mentored by people on the other side of the country, or even the world, breaking down geographical barriers inside enterprises. For the first time, companies are breaking down global silos and connecting employees through mentorship to learn from one another.
- Mentors and mentees can use the site to send messages, display their calendars, and organise meetings. If the mentor and mentee are in separate time zones, this is extremely useful.
- Technology provides businesses with never-before-seen data, allowing them to immediately assess the impact of their programs and verify ROI. It also serves as a centre for mentorship inside your company. You can centralise all things mentoring on a platform, making it more accessible and scalable, rather than relying on email or different pdfs and spreadsheets.
- Mentoring software can improve communication between program participants and administrators, in addition to mentor and mentee engagement. Admins will be able to send emails, surveys, and other types of contact from a single location.
- Mentors and mentees can use the cloud to access important documents at any time during the mentoring relationship. For all parties, reports may be created based on the relationship's growth. This aids the organization in determining the mentoring program's succes.

- The mentor pool is optimised for the mentee's individual aims and objectives using software. This allows the mentor-mentee connection to focus only on the needs of the mentee.
- Mentor training is essential for effective mentorship because it ensures that all participants understand the program. It also gives mentors and mentees the tools they need to set objectives and measure their progress.
- The benefit of revamping your mentorship programs digitally is that you may begin to fill in some of these gaps. Mentoring software keeps track of sign-ups, matches, sessions, skills, engagement, and progress, so you don't have to hunt down information or comments from your employees.
- Every element of communication, including mentoring, has been transformed by digital. It's levelled the playing field, allowing leaders, up-and-comers, and everyone in between to have more access to people and ideas than ever before.
- With virtual meetings, you can talk to your mentor from anywhere you are by picking up the phone or opening your laptop. This flexibility also allows more individuals to engage in the program because there are fewer restrictions on where they may participate or how they can get there.
- Mentors choose their mentees, and mentors choose their mentees. Digital tools, technologies, and apps such as social networking platforms, Skype, and the What's App program, among others, might make it easier for mentees and mentors to communicate, especially given hectic schedules, time zones, and other factors.
- Many times, the appointed mentor, sponsor, and HR leader were difficult to contact, and having tools that allowed for real-time communication would have been extremely beneficial.
- Although most mentoring programs include regular meetings throughout the program, you may wish to check in with your mentor at any time. When you have a quick query or need guidance regarding a specific problem at work or school, online chat or direct messaging may be a useful tool.

- Mentoring software may assist big programs in keeping track of members, progress, and overall program goals. One way that technology may help an organization is by reducing the amount of time and effort required from program administrators.
- Consider mentorship programs that aim to bring individuals together from different parts of the country or the world. Unless you want to spend a lot of money on vacation, this is only achievable with technology and an online mentorship program.
- Even for mentors and mentees who prefer to meet in person, there are instances when the flexibility of technology guarantees that the connection may continue even if an in-person encounter isn't possible—due to sickness, travel, or a jam-packed schedule.

While most training sessions take place in person, mentoring software can help with virtual training. The main point to remember is that convenience is important. Your program attendees can focus on the tasks at hand since technology takes the legwork out of mentoring. It is frequently a beneficial investment because it helps both the individual and the company. All mentorship programs benefit greatly from technology. However, there are particular situations in which a company should absolutely deploy mentoring technology. Here are some characteristics that a company in need of mentoring software may possess.When starting a mentoring program, the size of the company or program is one of the most important factors to consider when deciding whether or not to employ software. The greater the program, the more software is required. Admins are frequently busy and in high demand, so any software that might help them save time is beneficial. The variety of purposes will make the shift to employing technology easy and efficient, from simplicity and comfort to optimum mentor matches. Technology is advancing at a breakneck speed. Newcomers entering the sector may face a variety of obstacles and trends that they could not have imagined while in school. It may make all the difference in their job success if they have an experienced IT veteran at their side to show them the ropes and assist them in adapting. LinkedIn is a great place to look for mentors. I would urge young workers to look for profiles of their *"future selves"* and gently ask for career guidance from such people. From there, the connection can flourish.

Your Mentor Your Role Model

Being a mentor and a role model may be incredibly fulfilling and valuable. On a larger scale, a role model demonstrates leadership behaviours that others look to for direction and can learn from. A mentor fulfils a similar aspirational function but also works one-on-one with you to teach, challenge, and push you to reach your full potential. Professionals, in my opinion, should prioritise building good mentorships, which are more personal than serving as role models. Being a mentor, in my opinion, is the best way to help a colleague succeed in their career. Furthermore, good mentorship should enable a mentor to serve as a role model for the greater business community. Being a role model and a mentor at the same time may be highly rewarding. Mentorship, in the end, is a win-win situation for all parties involved and is based on meaningful interactions — all of which may happen in our present new normal. The connection is beneficial for up-and-coming professionals seeking career counselling, since some may be struggling during uncertain times and would benefit significantly from advice or a more experienced approach. If you don't have a mentor or mentee, I recommend reaching out to someone you like, even if it's only for a virtual cup of coffee, to start laying the basis for a future mentor-mentee connection. If your company is working to increase diversity in leadership positions, ensuring that mentees have equitable access to good mentors should be a top priority. Early-career professionals who do not work in the corporate headquarters are less likely to "run into" senior management and form business mentorship ties as a result. According to research, sharing a goal with a mentor who can hold us accountable increases our chances of achieving it by 70%. A mentoring culture is one in which employees emphasise personal growth, information exchange, and goal setting. Mentorship can help employees throughout the company feel more engaged and meaningful during National Mentoring Month, and we could all use a little more purpose in this time of national lockdown. Mentorship may serve as both a learning and development tool for improving skills and knowledge, as well as a health and wellness tool. Mentorship creates human connection, improves mental health, and combats isolation, which is why it has been a priority for so many organizations in the last year.

Organizational Challenges

In an increasingly distant and screen-dependent work environment, organizations have a challenge: how to preserve the benefits of face-to-face relationship-building and communication amongst employees. This is particularly problematic for organizational roles that rely heavily on relationships, such as mentoring. A crisis like this one only emphasises the need for companies to focus on developing the next generation of leaders. Due to the possibility that the pandemic could affect different places for months, organizations cannot afford to put their mentorship programs on hold, nor can they allow physical distance to be an impediment to individuals meeting. Rather than rejecting the use of technology, businesses may incorporate it into their mentoring programs to strengthen the bonds between mentor and mentee.

Flipside Of Tech Based Mentoring

- Nonverbal signals and other communication nuances are critical in mentoring since it's difficult for mentor and mentee couples to build rapport and trust without them. A virtual conference using Zoom, Skype, or other comparable video conferencing software preserves virtually all of the benefits of a face-to-face meeting without the trip.
- An essential client meeting or personal obligation may take precedence over a face-to-face appointment with one's mentor or mentee at times.

- Occasionally, though, organizations unintentionally disfavour some mentees. Being in a different geographic region, for example, might be a disadvantage in companies that rely on informal mentorship.
- All participants may be matched and connected via a platform, several firms have used mentoring software to manage their mentoring programs electronically. Businesses have been able to expand their mentorship activities further than ever before thanks to platforms like these. That is, it is not merely a band-aid solution, but rather an upgrade over the old method of doing things.
- Mentoring software, which allows mentor-mentee couples to be matched regardless of geographic location or other characteristics that aren't based on career potential, can help organizations democratise access to mentors.
- When businesses provide an online mentoring platform to aid mentoring, and mentees have equitable access to the mentoring software, web conferencing, and an internet connection, many of the disparities around mentoring evaporate.

More individuals can join your mentoring program thanks to online mentoring, which means there's a larger pool of people to match with, boosting the odds of better matching and increased involvement. This also broadens the scope of the program's knowledge and skills. Mentors and mentees are no longer limited by the abilities and expertise of those who share their cubicles or offices. People who participate in virtual mentorship programs have access to a wider range of individuals from various regions and backgrounds. People are exposed to other cultures and ideas, which can lead to a greater variety of thinking, innovation, and development via online mentorship programs.

Flipside Of Online Mentoring

- While there are numerous advantages to online mentoring, it's also crucial to be mindful of the drawbacks of a virtual program.

Communication is hampered by the inability to understand body language and facial expressions. This can occasionally result in a lack of chemistry. Fortunately, this may be avoided by giving mentors and mentees access to a number of communication methods, as well as the opportunity to use video whenever possible.

- Changing time zones can be a difficult obstacle to overcome. It might be difficult to have fruitful interactions when a mentee is in the morning and a mentor is in the evening. If this is the case for your program, make sure your participants are aware of the variations and are prepared to plan accordingly, such as by pre-queuing questions.
- If this is the case for your program, make sure your participants are aware of the differences and plan accordingly, whether it's through pre-queuing questions or finding a time that works best for both people.
- Technology may provide the greatest obstacle. As we all know, technology does not always function as we would like. Participants in online mentoring might feel frustrated by technological difficulties. When technology fails, email, direct messages, and phone calls can be used to complement video meetings. Here are a few more pointers to help you run a successful online mentorship program.
- You may only require some words of encouragement at times. In these sorts of scenarios, mentors and mentees can communicate through their online program, email, or SMS. Slack, Microsoft Team, LinkedIn, email, or the chat facilities within your mentoring platform are all good possibilities.
- Of course, if the participants in your program are in close enough proximity, you don't have to pick between online mentoring and in-person meetings. They can do a little bit of both, creating a deep human connection while reaching their business or personal goals through both in-person encounters and technology.

- However, adopting something as personal as mentoring and making it work online is not without its difficulties. Employees working from home may have harmed mentoring programs in terms of matching participants, maintaining track of connections, and assessing effects. This is where technology plays a role.

Summing Up

Mentorship is one of the most effective and influential methods for assisting a person in gaining experience, learning new skills, developing, and eventually growing in their profession. Technology has increased the flexibility with which mentors and mentees can connect and stay connected, just as it has in our businesses, schools, and society at large. Progressive companies are using technology, such as artificial intelligence (AI), to build talent marketplaces. Employers can use new technologies and trends to complement and expand traditional mentoring programs. When organizations use technology like online conferencing, mentors and mentees can continue to strengthen their connection even when in-person visits aren't possible. Using mentoring software, mentors and mentees no longer have to work in the same building. Virtual mentoring allows employees to be mentored by people on the other side of the country, or even the world. Mentoring software with matching capabilities provides mentorships a leg up on the competition in terms of compatibility. Digital tools, technologies, and apps such as social networking platforms, Skype, and the What's App program, among others, might make it easier for mentees and mentors to communicate. Mentoring programs that aim to bring individuals together from different parts of the country or the world can benefit from technology. In an increasingly distant and screen-dependent work environment, organizations have a challenge: how to preserve the benefits of face-to-face relationship-building. This is particularly problematic for roles that rely heavily on relationships, such as mentoring. Businesses may incorporate technology into their mentoring programs to strengthen bonds between mentor and mentee. People who participate in virtual mentorship programs have access to a wider range of individuals from various regions and backgrounds.

CHAPTER TEN

ORGANIZATIONAL CAPABILITY BUILDING

"Mentors have a way of seeing more of our faults that we would like. It's the only way we grow."

- George Lucas, American Film Director, Producer.

Mentoring programs are one of the most effective and least expensive methods for a firm to foster employee loyalty and engagement. High turnover rates can be decreased, productivity can be boosted, and your team's skill set can be broadened. Mentorship in the workplace has many benefits. According to statistics, mentoring is one of the most useful and successful growth opportunities a business can provide its workers. Having a trustworthy and experienced mentor give direction, encouragement, and support may provide a mentee with a wide range of personal and professional advantages, which can lead to greater job performance. Mentorship benefits everyone participating in the program, including the host organization. Mentoring decreases turnover considerably. Your team's abilities have improved. Mentorships and other career development programs can help your team members improve the talents they bring to the table. Workplace mentoring programs assist both the mentor and the mentee to develop soft skills. These programs can also assist high-performing individuals in reaching their full potential within your firm. Investing in a workplace mentorship program allows your firm to reap the benefits of the beneficial influence. However, if you let the hustle of reopening your office push your mentoring program to the backburner until a later date, you will miss out on these advantages. You will also have to start from scratch and rebuild your workplace mentorship program if you decide to discontinue it. Turnover costs US firms almost $1 trillion every year on average. Employee replacement costs are astronomically expensive. According to Gallup, the cost of replacing an employee might be as much as two times the employee's income or more. In the oil and gas industry, replacing highly specialised personnel can cost up to 400% of their salary. According to the Bureau of Labor Statistics report for 2021, the current turnover rate is 57.3 percent. With nearly 3 million Americans quitting their jobs every month, it's clear that businesses are having trouble keeping their staff. According to a 2019 CNBC/ SurveyMonkey Workplace Happiness Survey, more than four out of every ten workers without a mentor considered quitting their job in the previous three months.Mentorship, on the other hand, has been shown to be an effective way to reduce turnover. Mentees (72%) and mentors (69%) had significantly higher retention rates than workers who did not participate in the mentoring program (49%). By investing in a workplace mentorship program, you may demonstrate to employees that you care about their professional growth. This is an excellent approach to increasing employee loyalty while decreasing high turnover rates. Employee productivity is increased via mentorship. Mentorships assist people in feeling happy at work. This motivates them to work harder and take pride in their work.

Another Gallup poll showed that mentoring programs are one of numerous strategies to retain and engage 94 percent of millennials at work. Because millennials prioritise employment that has a clear value and offers an opportunity for personal or professional advancement, this is the case. Mentors provide millennial employees with the assistance and guidance they require to advance. In a new Accountemps analysis, 93 percent of workers polled said goal setting is vital to their job performance, yet for some professionals, such meetings with supervisors never happen. Some companies make the mistake of allowing new employees to shadow older employees in the hopes that important information will be communicated organically. Furthermore, according to Brad Johnson, co-author of the book "The Elements of Mentoring," over fifty years of study reveals that people who have exceptional mentors do better and have higher performance ratings than those who try to do it on their own. Mentorship is a two-way street. Employees require friendships at work in order to thrive. People who have close ties with their peers are 50% happier. They're also seven times more likely to be enthusiastic about their jobs.

Organizations benefit from workplace mentoring programs in a variety of ways, including:

1. Increased employee engagement by communicating to all employees that the company's leadership is prepared to invest in them.

2. Lower turnover rate because it encourages staff retention, which can result in lower turnover rates. 18. As a result of one-on-one engagement, training expenditures are lower.

3. Development of your talent's skills and improves the efficacy of talent recruitment initiatives. New employees are aware of the company's professional advancement options.

4. Increased workplace diversity

5. Increase productivity and earnings for organization. Implementing a mentoring program will raise an organization's productivity since mentorship, when done correctly, helps a mentee focus on their strengths and shortcomings while also boosting their confidence and performance. Mentoring increased productivity in 67 percent of organizations. Employee development is central to mentorship. Employee development opportunities are the second most significant factor in determining engagement.

6. Assists employees in meeting their talent development objectives, such as succession planning and good leadership development and is able to tap into the strength of natural leadership.

Mentorship in the workplace is a common approach for organizations to effectively incorporate new employees into the firm. However, these initiatives can and should be much more than a tool for onboarding. Strong mentorship programs not only benefit new recruits but also serve to foster an open, welcoming culture that encourages all employees to share their ideas for enhancing the organization. You'll need data to make a solid match. Creating a questionnaire that questions interested workers about their career goals, communication styles, and what they want in a mentor or mentee is one method to gather information. Mentor-mentee relationships that work are ones in which the members share common interests and personalities, as well as complementing aims.

If you put mentoring on the back burner, you risk losing all of these advantages, which may be tough to regain in the future. Consider that if you chose to restart your workplace mentorship program, you would be beginning from scratch. If your company has already invested in a mentoring program, it is critical to keep the momentum going for both the participants and the organization. Some companies make the mistake of allowing new employees to shadow older employees in the hopes that important information will be communicated organically. You'll need data to make a solid match. Creating a questionnaire that questions interested workers about their career goals, communication styles, and what they want in a mentor or mentee is one method to gather information.

Carol Dweck summarises her findings about the Organizational Growth Mindset into the following:

"Individuals who believe their talents can be developed (through hard work, good strategies, and input from others) have a growth mindset. They tend to achieve more than those with a more fixed mindset (those who believe their talents are innate gifts). This is because they worry less about looking smart and they put more energy into learning."

Mentorship: An Organizational Thought Process

Mentor-mentee relationships that work are ones in which the members share common interests and personalities, as well as complementing aims. Make mentoring a priority in your company's culture. Promote it during the hiring process, begin pairing new hires with mentors during orientation, and ensure that the pairings are given the resources they need to succeed. This necessitates extensive preparation, internal marketing, training, and follow-up. Ensure that top-level executives promote the program, underline its relevance, and are active participants. Maintain straightforward, uncomplicated, and upbeat communication. Make it clear that involvement is entirely optional, but emphasise the value of mentoring for both professional development and the company's bottom line. After launch, don't expect the application to operate on autopilot. Inquire about each participant's input on a frequent basis, and look for ways to enhance processes. Make a point of gathering success stories and testimonials in order to promote the program in the future. Mentoring programs and relationships differ not just from one company to the next, but also from one person to the next. It's critical, though, that everyone understands that mentor is not the same as supervisor. Mentors provide advice and assistance rather than assigning tasks or telling mentees how to execute their professions.

Tweet: Rahul Bajaj believed that women micro entrepreneurs can fuel job creation in rural areas when given appropriate financial support and mentoring. With his support, Bharatiya Yuva Shakti Trust has created hundreds of women Grampreneurs across all regions.

Need To Design Your Formal Mentorship Program

Business analyst Leticia shares, "Until I joined McKinsey, I did not know the difference between mentors and sponsors. I learned quickly that mentors are the people you'll reach out to for advice, whenever you feel bad or have to make a difficult decision, they will provide you guidance, or at least emotional comfort. Sponsors, on the other hand, are the ones who will proactively create opportunities for you to advance in your career, they'll push you to expand your limits and provide coaching to develop professional skills."

Do you want to know how to start a mentorship program? That's fantastic. Mentorship is a tried-and-true method for both mentees and mentors to achieve rich learning and growth.Any mentorship program should begin with the following two key questions:

1. What prompted you to start this program?
2. What does it mean to be successful for both the participants and the organization?

Convert your vision into SMART goals that are specific, measurable, achievable, relevant, and time-bound. Objectives provide program participants with direction, define program key performance indicators (KPIs), and explain why organizational leaders should support the program. Mentorship programs that work include structure as well as freedom. Structure provides participants with a mentoring procedure to follow, which is essential for achieving productive learning that meets established objectives. Flexibility is also necessary to meet varied individual mentoring requirements based on learning objectives, preferences, and learning styles. You won't have to guess who'll be the best fit for a new role or a promotion to a higher level of management. It relieves the stress of potential hiring errors and increases your chances of retaining outstanding staff. It can significantly reduce the revolving door of employees, which is both costly and disruptive to the company. A formal mentorship program allows you to focus important resources on things that can help you expand your business while reducing the time and money you spend on recruiting. Last but not least, mentorship isn't just for new hires. Mentors should be available at all levels of the organization, including the most senior executives. According to a PeopleFluent survey, 78 percent of millennials reported that participating in a mentoring program helped them feel more involved with their company. Furthermore, BambooHR discovered that providing "an employee buddy or mentor" was one of the most critical things a new employee required to come up to speed and start contributing quickly for 56 percent of new recruits.

Even the world's finest entrepreneurs, as evidenced by the examples above, require mentoring in order to shine brighter. Naveen Tewari, the founder and CEO of InMobi Group, India's first unicorn, was coached by Dr. Tarun Khanna, a Harvard Business School professor. Professor Khanna has researched how entrepreneurship may help emerging markets flourish socially and economically. His thoughts helped him see the bigger picture of the work we were doing. When he was driving InMobi, it showed him the value of dreaming big as an entrepreneur and solving large issues. The learning that began a decade ago has continued with Prof Khanna joining on InMobi's board. *"The experience and expertise of a long-time mentor like Prof. Khanna is invaluable for the company", he added.*

In an another story Bill Gates met Warren Buffet for the first time in July 1991, albeit unwillingly. Buffet is still one of Bill Gates' closest friends and mentors after 30 years. Business, economics, politics, international events, and philanthropy bring the two together. During Mark Zuckerberg's early days as an entrepreneur, Steve Jobs was his go-to person. On Jobs' request, Zuckerberg visited a temple in Uttarakhand and spent a month in India to see how people interacted. He had a greater understanding of the significance and relevance of his venture as a result of the experience. Furthermore, Sir William Crookes was an excellent experimenter, the inventor of the vacuum tube, and the discoverer of helium. Sir William Crookes was a chemist and physicist who studied at London's Royal College of Chemistry. After the discovery of the vacuum tube in 1875, he was regarded as a pioneer. He then invented the Crookes radiometer, which is still sold as a novelty item today. The radiometer, also known as a light mill, is made up of an airtight glass bulb with a partial vacuum inside of it. He was also a very spiritual individual who experimented with the paranormal on a regular basis. Someone as astute as him had to be on to something. Do you know that Nikola Tesla admired him and learned a lot from him? He was inspired by him and pursued his studies. Crookes, for his part, stood by Tesla's side, protecting him when the world turned against him at one point. Following up on Crookes‘ findings, Tesla discovered that Radiant the Mentoring Manager could also transmit electrostatic charges.

Important Aspects Of Good Mentorship Program

When employees’ own needs and the needs of the organization are in sync, they are happy, engaged, and productive. Salary and benefits may be sufficient to entice top talent into the door, but they will not be sufficient to retain or motivate them to do their best work. Employees attain their full potential when their employment provides intrinsic incentives, such as the satisfaction of doing important work that contributes to their personal and professional growth. The most important aspect of a good mentoring program is that it is human-oriented rather than bureaucratic. Pairing an employee with the correct mentor, according to **Tammy Allen**, author of Designing Workplace Mentor Programs, is the trickiest part of mentoring and the one we know the least about. Some organizations employ algorithms similar to those employed by dating sites, while others employ more haphazard approaches. Mentors should be aware that their time is valuable and that mentoring helps both parties. Furthermore, a Harvard Business Review survey of 30 professional organizations found that mentorship programs can easily become monotonous and bureaucratic in a hypercompetitive industry. One of the most amazing aspects of a successful mentoring program is the extent to which beneficial ripple effects may be felt. Mentorship improves an organization by increasing employee happiness and retention while also assisting the mentee’s personal and professional development.

A good workplace mentoring program should give continual assistance for each stage of the employee life cycle, regardless of where the individual is in the mentoring journey. It is critical that an administrator communicates with both mentors and mentees on a frequent basis to assess how their match and process are progressing. There will be occasions when one of the participants does not believe it is effective. At this stage, an administrator can assist in defining and resolving the issue, which may entail dissolving the match and forming a new one. Although tracking communication may appear to be a time-consuming chore, it will be made easier if you use a mentoring software tool. Program administrators can track emails and meetings using mentoring software. Although tracking communication may appear to be a time-consuming chore, it will be made easier if you use a mentoring software tool. Program administrators can track emails and meetings using mentoring software. It can also make it easier to remain in touch with participants.A detailed case study at Sun Microsystems is a nice example:

• Employees who participated in the program were five times more likely to advance in their pay grade, and mentors advanced even faster.

• Mentors were promoted five times more than non-mentees, while mentees were promoted six times more. Mentees (72%) and mentors (69%) had significantly higher retention rates than non-participating personnel (49%). Mentoring programs increased minority presence in management by 9 percent to 24 percent, according to Cornell University's School of Industrial and Labor Relations (compared to 2 percent to 18 percent with other diversity initiatives), according to the same study.boosted minorities' and women's promotion and retention rates by 15 percent to 38 percent when compared to non-mentored employees.

A strong mentorship program is a smart way to link your employees' personal goals with the goals of your company. Your workplace culture will thrive if those two interests are aligned. As a result, talent and opportunity marketplaces have become an essential tool for employees who still need to engage with managers and mentors throughout the organization's ecosystem.

Building Mentorship Culture In An Organization

A mentoring culture allows firms to bring on board not only profitable but also fascinating ideas, boosting their innovation quotient and giving them a competitive advantage. However, how will they make the transition from management to mentorship? Management's approach has long since vanished. The old approach to leading a team no longer works, especially as the younger generation enters the job. Leaders must recognise the peculiarities of the younger generation, as well as the reality that they are naturally gifted in certain areas, such as technology. This acknowledgement is the first step toward mentorship from management.

Prahlad Kakar, AD Film Director, Founder Genesis Film Production said at the recently held People Matters Total Rewards and Wellness Conclave 2019, "Mentorship is not about telling people what to do. It is about partnering."

Prahlad Kakar adds, "Mentorship is a two-way process, you both learn and teach. In fact, mentors often learn more than they teach." The Founder of Genesis Film Production spoke on the topic "Management to Mentorship" at the People Matters Total Rewards and Wellness Conclave 2019. On the topic of "Management to Mentorship," founder of Genesis Film Production, spoke at Mentored mentees have a 50% higher retention rate than those who are not mentored. Mentorship, in fact, has a considerably bigger influence on employee retention than compensation increases.

HR Role In Organizational Mentorship

Mentorship is one of the most underappreciated and underutilizedd talent management techniques. Mentorship has the potential to help individuals for a lifetime. According to a recent study by HR.Com, The State of Coaching and Mentoring 2020, as firms try to replace the informal interactions that existed before the epidemic, mentoring will rise dramatically over the next two years, according to a recent study by HR.Com. According to the report, the present mentorship is useless. The problem that firms face is establishing and maintaining a mentorship program that will improve performance and engagement, as well as profit and creativity. Mentoring also boosts *"organizational citizenship behaviour,"* which means individuals treat each other well and help one another, according to Ellen Esher, author of *"Power Mentoring: How Successful Mentors and Protégés Get the Most Out of Their Relationships."*

Mentoring in a VUCA environment

Welcome to the VUCA world if you're wondering why tactics or strategies that seemed to work in the past don't seem to work today, or why certain activities don't have the expected outcomes. VUCA is an acronym that stands for Very Urgent Critical Action. Uncertainty, chaos, and ambiguity characterise this situation. And there are no predictable responses in a VUCA environment. So, in a VUCA environment, how do you mentor? Mentoring in a VUCA world is less about giving solutions and more about assisting them in finding answers. In this VUCA environment where there are no predictable solutions, mentoring is about assisting your mentee in becoming more comfortable with not having all the answers and giving them the courage to find the answers on their own. A business will specify outcomes that they believe will be the consequence of workplace mentoring at the start of any mentoring program. It is critical that these be documented and that there be a means to measure the results. For example, if a company is launching a mentoring program to increase worker diversity, it may keep track of how many leadership roles are held by minorities. If the number rises as a result of the mentoring program's execution, the mentorship experience can be considered a success. Whatever the aims of your organization's workplace mentoring program are, it is critical that the results be monitored on a regular basis. Whatever the aims of your organization's workplace mentoring program are, it is critical that the results be monitored on a regular basis. This might assist you in determining the program's level of success. If the program is not producing the anticipated results, you may need to make changes to the mentorship experience.

Best Practices In Mentorship

Following a set of best practises will guarantee that your mentoring program is as effective as possible for both your mentees and your company.

- Establish ground rules and expectations. One of the difficulties with mentorship programs is that mentees sometimes do not know what to anticipate from the experience. They may turn to mentors to set their goals for them, or they may realise that the people involved do not agree on how frequently to meet.

- Creating a voluntary, employee-driven mentorship system can assist in avoiding these dangers. We're upfront about the time commitment required at Dataminr, and we ask that participants meet at least once a month for six months.
- Participants go through a systematic application process and training program, and we provide tactical templates and a monthly budget for off-site sessions, resulting in a more tailored and effective experience.
- Whether these leaders provide a budget, advocate for workers to participate, or encourage other senior leaders to sign up, leadership support is the lifeblood of these sorts of initiatives and demonstrates to employees how much senior management values their success.
- Collect feedback as soon as possible and as frequently as possible.Aside from their monthly meetings, program participants should be encouraged to share their thoughts on their experiences. Companies that do not set key performance indicators (KPIs) and gather feedback are passing up an opportunity to optimise for better results. Dataminr, for its part, collects both qualitative and quantitative feedback every eight weeks through three feedback sessions in each 6-month program. We advocate conducting brief questionnaires to measure participant satisfaction, determine how much they appreciate the program, and determine how much it affects their job.
- Assign your program's responsibility to a single team.A mentoring program must be part of a certain team inside your business in order to function well. It is up to these team members to advocate for the program, assess its progress, and accept responsibility for its outcomes. This job frequently overlaps with the activities of human resources (HR). HR (or a comparable people-focused team) can pilot its success by

supporting the application process, finding meaningful connections, supervising the program's orientation training, and ensuring that participants prioritise their engagement.

- If your mentoring program hasn't succeeded in the past, it's likely because it lacked the structure and accountability required to foster the proper degree of participation. By implementing these best practises, you can transform this opportunity for learning and growth into a strategy for increasing employee happiness, engagement, and retention—and, as a result, position your business for future growth.

Summing Up

Mentorship programs are one of the most effective and least expensive methods for a firm to foster employee loyalty and engagement. High turnover rates can be decreased, productivity can be boosted, and your team's skill set can be broadened through mentorship. Strong mentorship programs not only benefit new recruits but also serve to foster an open, welcoming culture that encourages all employees to share their ideas for enhancing the organization. Make mentoring a priority in your company's culture. Promote it during the hiring process and ensure that new hires are matched with mentors. Maintain straightforward, uncomplicated, and upbeat communication. Make it clear that involvement is entirely optional, but emphasise its value. Mentors should be aware that their time is valuable and that mentoring helps both parties. Employees are less likely to become stagnant or disengaged at work if they continue to learn and grow alongside the company.Mentorship is typically created informally within a corporation. Internal mentors can help mentees think about career options, negotiate delicate political circumstances, and adjust to a changing culture. External mentors are frequently unbiased and offer objective perspectives on professional choices because they are not limited by the limits or expectations of an organization. Mentorship is a tried-and-true method for both mentees and mentors to achieve rich learning and growth. A formal mentorship program allows you to focus important resources on things that can help you expand your business. It also reduces the time and money spent on recruiting new employees. The most important aspect of a good mentoring program is that it is human-oriented rather than bureaucratic. Some organizations employ algorithms similar to those employed by dating sites, while others employ more haphazard approaches.

CHAPTER ELEVEN

REVERSE MENTORSHIP A SILVER BULLET

"To stand out in the market, we need to reverse-engineer what makes the market so alive!" –Jack Welch

Reverse mentoring is a learning relationship in which senior executives or experienced staff are matched with younger employees who then impart their knowledge of technology, social media, and current workplace trends. Unlike traditional mentoring, in which the mentor is always a senior professional who can pass on experience without fear of resentment from the mentee, reverse mentoring fosters an atmosphere in which knowledge and ideas may easily flow and the organisational hierarchy is flattened. When a younger employee actively participates in educating, providing criticism, or imparting valuable expertise to a senior counterpart, this is referred to as *reverse mentoring*. It's a two-way street that illustrates that younger workers have experience and viewpoints that older employees and the organization can benefit from. As a result, both junior and senior members function as mentors and mentees simultaneously. According to a recent Forbes survey, 85 percent of top executives say diverse and inclusive workforces are critical to innovation.

Reverse mentorship is becoming more popular as a way to include employees, particularly Millennials, in the process. It allows younger employees to feel like they are a part of the mentoring process. When a Baby Boomer employee approaches a Millennial employee to learn more about coding or social media, for example, it establishes trust. As a result, each participant takes on the role of being an active part of the organization. When it comes to organisational hierarchy, traditional business mentorship favours the status quo. By mentoring others, top leadership is given even more influence and reverence. Reverse mentoring contributes to the creation of a more inclusive company culture. Reverse mentorship fosters social skills, diversity skills, and cross-cultural competency in the executive team, where they are most required. When he was CEO of GE, Jack Welch was acknowledged as being one of the early users of reverse mentorship. Welch, employed a magic elixir known as "Reverse Mentoring" to set his company apart from its competitors. To understand the demands of a fresh new economy, he had to bridge the technological knowledge gap between generations. chose a junior employee to be his mentor and then ordered that 500 of his executives choose a reverse mentor. He advised senior executives to learn from junior professionals about how to use and navigate the internet, as well as about emerging methods of reaching the target demographic. Since then, several major corporations, such as HP, The Hartford, Cisco, and Coca-Cola, have launched reverse mentorship programs. At Caterpillar the organization's mentoring initiatives have been a success, so they've introduced a reverse mentoring component in the shape of ERGs.

Tana Utley, Vice President of Caterpillar's Large Power Systems Division, remarked that Millennials approach the workplace differently than previous generations, which is important for top executives to grasp.

Growing Strategic Need Of Reverese Mentoring

Workplaces are evolving to encourage more cooperation and connection. The article discusses the significance of mentoring as well as its new and enhanced form, reciprocal or reverse mentoring. Reverse Mentoring: a potent tool, a silver bullet for workplace engagement and empowerment. PwC: With an emphasis on diversity and inclusion, PwC has implemented reverse mentoring programmes throughout its global offices. According to its participants, it has had a beneficial influence on diversity, skill development, and a learning culture inside the organization. Just as standard corporate mentoring broadens the mentee's perspective by assisting them in seeing the larger organisational picture, reverse mentoring assists executives in broadening their viewpoint by assisting them in better understanding the experiences of others. Bharti Airtel executives were at the same crossroads a few years ago, when they needed to conceive of fresh marketing methods but looked to have exhausted all of their promotional efforts. One of them had the brilliant notion of going *"Back to the Basics!"* He was essentially saying that the need of the hour was to gather feedback from the customers themselves. The decision to launch the reverse mentorship programme was a watershed event for the company! You've definitely observed the impact of workplace culture on overall enjoyment, retention, and productivity, whether you're a retiring CEO or a new graduate employee. *According to Peter Drucker, "culture eats strategy for breakfast."* Many instances of how reverse mentoring has aided huge organisations can be found online, but how do you market the concept such that leadership embraces it? A first step would be to start modestly. If you're having trouble fostering reciprocal or reverse mentoring within your business, try it on a mentor or coach outside of it. People like assisting others. It enables individuals to donate to others in areas they are familiar with and feel good about.

Mr. Jack Welch hired 500 young trainees to serve as mentors, teaching senior executives how to use the internet and conduct e-advertising. Jack demonstrated why reverse mentorship is the way of the future! Most people assume that a mentor-mentee relationship is one in which a mentor contributes his or her time only for the benefit of the mentee. Many young professionals are discouraged from finding mentors because they believe they are asking for too much time from mentors with nothing to offer in return. Furthermore, organisational outcomes increasingly encompass more than just financial and core strategic value; they are expanding to include purpose through social enterprise. Reverese Mentoring is an excellent approach to keep old executives up-to-date on the latest developments while also making the most of our demographic dividend. This is now being used by an increasing number of Indian organisations, with CEOs and senior management leading by example. *Sanjay Kapoor, Deputy CEO of Bharti Airtel said that he felt younger after every session and all the more geared up! Such new and fresh energy was infused through such gatherings and they realized that this activity kept them contemporary in vision.*

Making the workplace more just and inclusive is a difficult endeavour. A half-day workshop will not result in a long-term transformation of a company. To fulfil DE & I objectives, a number of techniques are required, including cultural change efforts, changing recruiting processes, and establishing employee resource groups. Reverse mentoring reverses standard corporate mentoring by making the more junior person the mentor and the more senior person the mentee. It contributes to DE & I projects in a variety of ways. It fosters an open culture in which younger workers are encouraged to offer ways for older employees to be more productive, such as *"I know of a better programme we can use for tracking action items,"* or *"Did you know there's a way we can all modify this paper at the same time?"*

For today's organisations, millennial retention is a major concern. Millennials are now the largest generation in the work market, and 43 percent of the demographic group want to leave their employment within the next two years, according to the 2018 Deloitte Millennial Survey. Do you know there's a method you can all change this document at the same time? However, just a third of Millennials believe their employers are successfully utilising their skills, and 42% say they are likely to resign due to a lack of development opportunities. According to Glassdoor research, the *"capacity to learn and grow"* is currently the primary driver of a company's employment brand among Millennials. Despite this, only one-third of Millennials believe their organisations make good use of their skills, and 42% expect to leave as a result. The figures show a historically high turnover rate, which is causing businesses to scramble to design and implement engagement measures. This generation expects flexible settings and socially responsible missions, as well as continual learning and transferrable skill development, personal fulfilment, and clear prospects for professional advancement—needs that reverse mentoring may help provide. The authors of *"The Gen Z Effect: The Six Forces Shaping the Future of Business,"* Thomas Koulopoulos and Dan Keldsen, believe that this is the case.Despite the fact that 51 percent of those 600 organisations have cross-generational teams, just 14 percent have a reverse mentorship programme in place. So, to enhance employee engagement and retention, company cultures must be relevant and compelling. Reciprocal mentorship is one method for improving individualised training for workers while also fostering an open atmosphere in which even junior employees feel appreciated. As a result, the corporation is both effective and regarded as a terrific place to work by its workers. In his book "Indian Unbound," Gurcharan Das stated that it was this unique approach that put Bharti Airtel on the leading edge. This has prompted many aspiring corporate executives to venture into the realm of "*Mentworking*" (the fusion of mentoring and networking)!

If there is a silver bullet for engaging your multigenerational team, reverse mentoring would be it. Reverse mentoring is a means to break down barriers between executives and junior employees, whether it's to understand how Millennials or GenZ think about work or learn about emerging trends. Because of the rapid progress of technology and social media, the younger generation is usually able to advise more senior staff. Not all knowledge comes with age. With the world changing at such a fast pace, it's no surprise that most HR departments will use their "network intelligence" to mentor a new face this year by leveraging their multigenerational workforce. Despite the fact that 83 percent of professionals want to be a part of a mentoring programme, just 29 percent of them work in organisations that provide one. Reverse mentorship fosters a variety of contexts in which people may interact openly, exchange insights, share ideas, and question legacy thinking. When a younger employee actively participates in educating, providing criticism, or imparting valuable expertise to a senior counterpart, this is referred to as "reverse mentoring." It's a two-way street that illustrates that younger workers have experience and viewpoints that older employees and the organisation can benefit from. As a result, both junior and senior members function as mentors and mentees simultaneously. When you choose to engage in reverse mentoring, you may also get useful information about your customer or employee demographic. You will also be displaying constant learning and, ideally, the great communication abilities that so many Millennials require. Since April 2021, Heineken has been operating a reverse mentorship programme on Together's platform. The outcomes have been spectacular. When asked, 86 percent of mentees (senior executives) said they wished to interact with more junior employees to learn new skills and experience the future generation of talent. According to Jeanette Gibson, Director of Social and Digital Marketing at Cisco Systems Inc., when the company started its Generation Y Reverse Mentoring Program around two years ago, it *"became a badge of honour."*

The time has come to let go of the attitudes of the past and usher in a new age of colearning! As someone correctly stated, "junior" and "senior" refer to the assignment, not the age! It may enable experienced workers to stay current with emerging technology for extended periods of time without the need for extra formal training. They can adapt to new workplace technologies and trends like social networking, phone messaging apps, crowdsourcing, and other new software. It has the capacity to transmit data. This time may be better spent informing more senior staff about what the younger generation values and expects from their organisation. It instils trust and gives new workers leverage. If the young mentors manage the situation well, they will gain essential leadership skills. The standard business mentoring strategy will not successfully move the needle on indicators of diversity, equality, and inclusion.

Mentorship, on the other hand, may be a strong tool to incorporate into a company's DE & I projects. Savvy organisations employ reverse mentoring to promote DE and I goals, rather than the typical mentoring framework. Reverse mentoring reverses standard corporate mentoring by making the more junior person the mentor and the more senior person the mentee. It backs DE & I.

Flipside Of Reverse Mentoring

- Trust, transparency, openness to learning, and compatibility are all required for effective outcomes. This partnership must achieve these requirements in order for the firm to stay up with the Joneses. If there is a personality mismatch, there may be consequences. While assisting their bosses with e-skills, younger interns must be compassionate, patient, and courteous.
- Likewise, the mentees in this scenario must be open and passionate throughout these sessions. Both must recognise that mentoring is a two-way street of mutual learning rather than a one-way street of information transmission.
- Some overseas businesses utilise a third party to monitor the success of all mentor-mentee couples in order to achieve effective outcomes. Both the mentor and the mentee submit reports on their partner's performance, which are then evaluated by the mediator.
- Consider having someone teach you something you believe you already know, such as leadership, rather than just mentoring you on social media.
- Reverse mentoring is a relatively new type of workplace mentorship, but it's growing in popularity as a means to link senior executives with the next generation of talent. Senior leaders may take on the role of students again and obtain a fresh perspective by turning the usual mentoring relationship on its head.
- Smaller organizations, on the other hand, may find it difficult to develop internal mentoring programmes since it is impossible to match a mentor and a mentee who do not have any form of

power relationship with each other and hence may have skewed impressions of others.

- One of the most important things is that it should be done with care so that no one feels like they're being told they're not performing their job well enough. Insulting long-serving employees poses a serious danger if not handled properly, or if the younger mentor fails to manage the problem responsibly.
- In a society that values on-the-job learning for all ages, the phrase "reverse mentoring" is antiquated and perhaps harmful.
- The word "mentor" itself is founded on an unconscious prejudice; it is based on the idea that "regular" mentoring (i.e., not reversed) comes only from colleagues who are older than their mentee. Therefore, it stands to reason that it is reversed when the mentor is younger or more junior than the mentee.
- From a legal standpoint, you may challenge the morality of using the term "reverse mentoring," which is predicated on age or seniority, which is, on average, tied to age.
- Due to the lack of objective justification—that is, the employer's being able to show a good reason for age discrimination—this could potentially leave the organisation open to cases of age discrimination where a younger or "junior" employee feels as if they are being treated less favourably if they are the mentor in a "reversed mentoring" relationship; they may perceive that they were initially seen as having nothing to offer in terms of mentoring.

How HR Can Support Reverse Mentoring

If the quantity of assignments or exercises your mentor wants you to do makes you feel overwhelmed, remember that wisdom does not always come with age. Meet three leaders and their Millennial workers, who are mentoring them. Keeping up with the dizzying speed of change as technology affects how organisations operate may be difficult. Fortunately, there is a simple, low-cost method to close the knowledge gap: tap into the abilities of your own Millennial employees—a generation that grew up surrounded by technological advancements in a world where change was the only constant.Reverse mentoring isn't a new concept, but it's a method that's especially pertinent in the digital era. Younger employees are partnered with executives to help them grasp and harness emerging trends in social media, mobile technology, and customer preferences. The secondary goal of reverse mentoring is to prepare young workers to become next-generation leaders. There aren't quite enough members of Generation X to replace such responsibilities as Baby Boomers retire in droves (about 10,000 adults born between 1946 and 1964 turn 65 every day). As a result, Millennials (those born between 1981 and 1997), the largest generation in the workforce, will be in charge of filling the vacancies. *"Embracing a reverse mentoring culture allows each generation to learn from and share their own unique experiences. Millennials, particularly Generation Z employees, have what we refer to as a "natural software attitude." "A software mentality,"* explains Nigel Heap, Regional Managing Director UK&I & EMEA, *"is a combination of embracing, understanding, and adopting technology, as well as adding human value to maximise the technology and infuse creativity."*

- Furthermore, because many Baby Boomers choose to stay at work longer than previous generations, keeping them productive and up-to-date is crucial to their success. Because of their strong desire to be heard and contribute more meaningfully to their professions, many businesses are enrolling Millennials in this endeavour. Reverse mentoring programmes come in a variety of shapes and sizes, but they all include one-on-one interactions in which a younger employee mentors an executive. The sessions are usually held once a month for six months to a year.
- There is no one-size-fits-all approach to reverse mentoring. The idea is that it must feel genuine to your culture.Some firms combine reverse mentoring with diversity efforts by pairing younger employees with senior executives who can assist them in developing their careers. By promoting examples and sharing

success stories, HR professionals may also help to develop informal arrangements. Even one-time gatherings can be beneficial in creating an atmosphere where individuals of different generations can reach out to assist one another.

- For example, marketing firm OgilvyOne Worldwide in New York City uses an informal structure to link executives with bright young talent in its Young Professional Network, which includes around 450 professionals under the age of 35 out of a staff of 5,800.
- According to Chaudhuri, HR can assist in the program's success by reminding CEOs of the benefits of lifelong learning and urging leaders to listen rather than talk. Programs that are enjoyable, adaptable, and do not take up too much time are also more likely to be effective. "If you walk in assuming you know everything, it's not going to be as beneficial," says mentee Dan Ohman, CEO of United Healthcare's central area, which employs 250,000 people. Having someone else take the lead and drive the conversation is a bit of a different experience. It's a terrific experience if you're receptive to it.While little study has been done on how reverse mentoring affects company goals, experts note that such programmes have been found to boost work satisfaction and engagement by connecting participants to the organisation.
- Some businesses additionally keep track of participant retention and mentor promotion rates.
- According to the Moving Ahead research, 87 percent of mentors and mentees feel empowered and have gained confidence as a result of their mentoring interactions.

My argument is that we all learn in different ways and that we can learn from anybody who offers the information, direction, and viewpoint we require to fill a knowledge or skill deficit. Accept it for what it is, rather than tarnishing it with ethically dubious titles. With all protections in place, the initiative is set to be a game changer for academic institutions suffering from stagnancy and lethargy. Mentors and mentees can develop new relationships that are both motivating and honest.

Summing Up

Unlike traditional mentoring, reverse mentoring fosters an atmosphere in which knowledge and ideas may easily flow. When a younger employee actively participates in educating, providing criticism, or imparting valuable expertise to a senior counterpart, this is referred to as reverse mentoring. Reverse mentoring assists executives in broadening their viewpoint by assisting them in better understanding the experiences of others. Just as standard corporate mentoring broadens the mentee's perspective by assisting them in seeing the larger organisational picture, reverse mentoring assists executives in broadening their viewpoint by assisting them in better understanding the experiences of others. Reverese Mentoring is an excellent approach to keep old executives up-to-date on the latest developments while also making the most of our demographic dividend. This is now being used by an increasing number of Indian organisations, with CEOs and senior management leading by example. Some overseas businesses utilise a third party to monitor the success of all mentor-mentee couples in order to achieve effective outcomes.

Conclusion

Plutarch once said, "The mind is not a vessel to be filled, but a fire to be kindled."

This, in my opinion, is the one that provides the most bang for the buck, given that it is not something that the organisation has mandated as a deliverable and is based on a relationship. Organic mentorship was once a very common part of corporate workplaces, but I believe it is now a unfortunately disappearing art. To hazard a few guesses, the reasons would be: Shorter tenures are used in situations where one of the two potential partners leaves before the professional relationship reaches a point where the mentoring structure can be applied. The development of a skilled mentor who possesses the specialised knowledge and scientific instruments necessary to give value to someone seeking professional advancement is an example. Individuals with younger ages and experience gaps performing manager and subordinate roles in fast-paced professional paths may not be well suited to a mentoring relationship. Professionals' concentration becomes limited to the current month or quarter, at best in light of today's business reality, and they lose sight of their own long-term growth requirements. Devoting head space, energy, and time to another's development is an agenda item that gets dropped easily at a time when all professionals are on a knife's edge. Whatever the reasons, the truth is that organisations are at a loss as this ad hoc mentoring process becomes less prevalent. This is something that anyone on the receiving end of mentorship will appreciate above all else in a world that is dynamic and demanding, considering the velocity of change all around us. Those who want to be mentored should be cautious and use the support sparingly when they put themselves up for mentorship. Treat it like a single-serving appetiser rather than a water fountain from which to drink. To put it another way, accept and enjoy the mentoring, but combine it with your own views and opinions as you move forward.Treat it as a virtuous deed or even meditation for those key leaders or mentors without whom mentoring would be impossible. It could be the ideal method for you to give back to the company or industry that helped you grow. Mentorship is becoming increasingly rare. It's in your capable hands to refresh it and support future leaders. Our mentors are the ones that light the fire in our hearts when it comes to business. They motivate us, assist us in difficult situations, and direct our paths. So it was: Hanuman needed to be reminded of his full potential and powers when he was most needed, and once he was, he went on to accomplish great things. When it comes to business, our mentors are the ones that kindle the fire in our hearts. They inspire us, help us through difficult times, and direct our paths. So it was: Hanuman needed to be reminded of his full potential and powers at a time when they were most needed, and once he was, he went on to great feats. We're all struggling with temporal compression, and the higher we climb the corporate ladder, the more filtered the data becomes. When you mentor strategically throughout the business, you get a sense of what's important, you acquire real-time data, and that, at the end of the day, is what will offer your company a competitive edge.

About The Author

Dr. Amit is the founder of Accumentor India, a consultancy firm set up by him in the human resource solution space, which is focused on developing processes for people. It offers consultancy in learning management, mentorship, performance coaching, training and development, psychometric analysis, HR processes and interventions. He was formerly the Director of Expertell Learning Point.

Dr. Amit Das is an experienced sales, training, and learning professional with more than 20 years of working history in the healthcare, medical devices, and learning management industries. Dr. Amit is a seasoned training professional with rich experience and a successful track record in aligning learning and training solutions to key business strategy with a strong focus on flawless execution excellence to facilitate individual, business divisional, and organizational performance. He keeps relentless focus on measuring training impact and ROI, people capability building graphs, training process governance, performance coaching, and strategic thinking. These have been some of his key individual success traits. His core capabilities include performance coaching, designing training and development frameworks and facilitation of technical skill building, psychometric assessment and analysis, competency framework development and assessments, content design and facilitation of soft skills and leadership programmes, E-Learning Platform development, Learning Management Systems, Learning Impact Measurement, Talent Analysis and Performance Management System Review, Performance Coaching and Counselling.

His interests are in the areas of leadership development, coaching competency, mentorship, and motivational complexities related to organizational issues. His hobbies include public speaking, content creation, and reading books. He has a Ph.D. and a Fellowship degrees in strategic learning, along with his first class degrees in PGDHRM & Corporate Laws from the top twenty business schools in India. He is a certified professional coach from U.K. He lives in Kolkata with his parents, wife, and son.

References For Reading

- Coaching and Mentoring at Work (2012) Developing Effective Practice By Mary Connor, Julia Pokora
- Micki Holliday's Coaching, Mentoring, and Managing, (2001) Breakthrough Strategies to Solve Performance Problems and Build Winning Teams.
- Coaching and Mentoring Supervision: The Complete Guide to Best Practice (Supervision in Context), 1st Edition (2012) by Tatiana Bachkiova et al.
- Mentoring and Coaching: A Lifetime for Teachers in a Multicultural Setting (2010) By Denise M. Gudwin, Magda D. Salazar-Wallace
- Laura Gail Lunsford's Starting, Supporting, and Sustaining (2016).
- Coaching and Mentoring: How to develop top talent and achieve stronger performance (2004), HBS Press.
- Mentoring, Coaching, and Collaboration: Special Edition (2008) by Dr. Jim Knight
- Successful Coaching and Mentoring Become an Effective Coach or Mentor Develop the key skills you need, benefit from a coaching programme, Share the Knowledge You Have Gained (2012) by Ken Lawson
- Coaching and Mentoring for Business (2014) by Grace McCarthy.
- Coaching, Counseling, and Mentoring: How to choose and use the right technique to boost employee performance (2007) by Florence M. Stone.
- 50 activities for coaching and mentoring (2010) by Donna Berry.
- Coaching, Mentoring, and Supervision (2012) by Anne Brockbank and Ian McGill
- From 2016 to 2022, HBR Magazines

- Human Capital Magazine 2015–2021
- Human Asia Magazine for 2019-2021
- Jonathan Passmore, David Peterson, and Teresa Freire's Wiley-Blackwell Handbook of the Psychology of Coaching and Mentoring (2016).
- In The Talent Code, greatness isn't born. It's great. Here's how 2009) by Daniel Coyle.
- John C. Maxwell's Mentoring 101: What Every Leader Needs to Know
- One Minute Mentoring, how to find and work with a mentor and why you will benefit from being one, by Ken Blanchard and Claire Diaz-Ortiz.
- Tony Dungy and Nathan Whitaker are the authors of "The Mentor Leader: Secrets to Building People and Teams That Win Consistently."
- The Mentor's Guide: Facilitating Effective Learning Relationships by Lois J. Zachary
- The Mentoring Manual: Your Step-by-Step Guide to Being a Better Mentor by Julie Starr
- Bridging Differences for Better Mentoring by Lisa Z. Fain and Lois J. Zachary
- 10 Steps to Successful Mentoring by Wendy Axelrod
- Mentoring Programs That Work by Jennifer Labin
- Elements of Mentoring: 75 Practices of Master Mentors by W. Brad Johnson
- Harvard Business Review: HBR Guide to Getting the Mentoring You Need (HBR Guide Series)
- Connecting: The Mentoring Relationships You Need to Succeed in Life (Paperback) by Paul D. Stanley
- Tony Dungy's The Mentor Leader: Secrets to Building People and Teams That Win Consistently, published in 2010.
- Finding a mentor, being a mentor: (2001) sharing our lives as women of God by Donna Otto
- Power Mentroing (2005) by Ellen A. Ensher.
- The Mentor's Guide: Facilitating Effective Learning

Relationships (2009) by Lois J. Zachary
- Modern Mentoring (2015) by Randy Emelo
- Mentoring: Confidence in finding a mentor and becoming one by Bobb Biehl
- Mentor Coaching: Effective Mentoring for the Personal and Professional Development of Young Adults by Terrice Thomas & Ann Rolfe
- Critical Mentoring: A Practical Guide by Torie Weiston-Serdan and Bernadette Sánchez
- Scott Jeffrey Miller's Master Mentors: 30 Transformative Insights from Our Greatest Minds

Printed by Libri Plureos GmbH in Hamburg, Germany